How to . . .

get the ...

COLES NOTES

Key Point

Basic concepts in point form.

Close Up

Additional hints, notes, tips or background information.

Watch Out!

Areas where problems frequently occur.

Quick Tip

Concise ideas to help you learn what you need to know.

Remember This!

Essential material for mastery of the topic.

Your guide to...
Pool

- 8-ball, 9-ball & 14.1
- Shots & strategies
- Rules & drills

ABOUT COLES NOTES

COLES NOTES have been an indispensable aid to students on five continents since 1948.

COLES NOTES now offer titles on a wide range of general interest topics as well as traditional academic subject areas and individual literary works. All COLES NOTES are written by experts in their fields and reviewed for accuracy by independent authorities and the Coles Editorial Board.

COLES NOTES provide clear, concise explanations of their subject areas. Proper use of COLES NOTES will result in a broader understanding of the topic being studied. For academic subjects, COLES NOTES are an invaluable aid for study, review and exam preparation. For literary works, COLES NOTES provide interesting interpretations and evaluations which supplement the text but are not intended as a substitute for reading the text itself. Use of the NOTES will serve not only to clarify the material being studied, but should enhance the reader's enjoyment of the topic.

© Copyright 2001 and Published by
COLES PUBLISHING. A division of Prospero Books
Toronto – Canada
Printed in Canada

Cataloguing in Publication Data
Hardt, Christina, 1962–

Your guide to … pool: 8-ball, 9-ball & 14.1;
shots & strategies; rules & drills

(Coles notes) ISBN
Written by Christina Hardt
ISBN 0-7740-0629-3

1. Pool (Game). I. Title. II. Series

GV891.H37 2001   794.7'3   C2001-930522-2

Publisher: Nigel Berrisford
Editing: Paul Kropp Communications
Book design: Karen Petherick, Markham, Ontario
IllustrationS: Colleen Lynch

Cover photo: Corbis

Manufactured by Webcom Limited
Cover finish: Webcom's Exclusive DURACOAT

Contents

Chapter One

A pool school primer

How hard can it be to roll a ball into a big hole with a long stick? Although the objective of pool is simple enough in theory, prepare for a formidable challenge in practice. Playing pool will offer moments of exhilaration and frustration. You'll be tempted to quit time and time again – but you won't. The game is also irresistible.

There are many reasons why people play and, consequently, varying degrees of dedication and discipline. Regardless of your skill level or goals, if you want to enjoy this game at any level you must master the basics: pool isn't fun unless you can pocket balls. You must learn to control the cue stick to pocket a ball, the cue ball to run a rack and, ultimately, the self-control to keep improving.

So before we start working on your game, let's cover some of the basics.

THE NAME OF THE GAME

Beginners and seasoned pool players alike have experienced confusion over billiard games and their various names. This is because billiards has a unique structure from other games.

Billiards is the official designation for the family of games played on a billiard table – with or without pockets. Some players use the word pool to mean billiards. You will also hear the carom disciplines called billiards, and learn how to execute pool shots called caroms and billiards. This is why the term **cue sports** is a welcome addition to the billiard lexicon – it eliminates confusion and includes everything.

1

Billiards or cue sports are broken down into three separate divisions – **pool**, **snooker** and **carom**; each division has its own sub-disciplines or games. Although the basics of each cue sport – pool, snooker and carom – are similar, the disciplines, equipment, rules and tactics are distinct.

Pool or **pocket billiards** (the upscale name) is a group of games played with a rack of either 15 or 9 numbered striped and solid balls on a table with pockets. Enjoyable at all levels, pool is a highly accessible cue sport – anyone can play. The tables are smaller, the balls bigger and the pockets are generally, shall we say, compassionate. Someone who has never held a cue before can sink a few balls – intentionally or unintentionally – and have a lot of fun doing it. The elements of luck and instant gratification give pool games like 8-ball and 9-ball tremendous appeal with beginners and social players.

Perhaps 8-ball's universal allure can be attributed to the fact that the object of the game is so simple: played with 15 numbered balls and a white cue ball, one player shoots the solid balls (numbered 1 through 7) while the other player shoots the stripes (9 through 15). Sink your group of balls, then the black 8-ball and you win. In fact, the time-honored game, which is also known as stripes and solids, is so popular that the black 8-ball itself has become a pop icon.

 Billiards (or cue sports) are recognized as sports – ones belonging to the Olympic family: in 1998 the International Olympic Committee (IOC) awarded the World Confederation of Billiard Sports (WCBS) permanent status.

IMAGE

Snooker and carom have long been hailed as "gentlemen's games." Played by the rich and royal, these cue sports continue to convey an image of well-mannered billiard players in tuxedos, elegant games rooms and the accoutrements of privilege: in a word, *respectability*.

Pool, on the other hand, had racked up quite a different connotation in North America. The family of games that got their name from the in-house betting pools became typecast as shady and delinquent. For a time, pool was very much a four-letter word – in the minds of certain moralists, at least.

Concerned players and industry members retaliated by launching a public relations juggernaut. This campaign was aimed at attracting women and families, a new breed of player for this beloved pastime, which they publicly referred to as *pocket billiards*.

Today, you don't have to call pool *pocket billiards* to know that it's a noble discipline. You can hone your skills in a club where the game's most respected players are on hand to continually astonish and mentor. Recreational players have also discovered that upscale billiard clubs, like golf courses, are fantastic places to release a day's stress or entertain business associates. Families with a home pool table enjoy hours of quality entertainment away from the television (unless pool's on TV, of course).

Acknowledged as "cool," it's fashionable – and slightly risqué – for some social pool players to boast about having put themselves through college *hustling* pool. Although these fish tales are a welcome barometer of pool's mainstream popularity, they still perpetuate a romantic image of hustling and sharking – the real animus behind pool's stigma. More often than not these terms are misunderstood and frequently misused.

Gambling or gaming, in moderation, is an acceptable part of many sports. Players who bet on their pool games do so primarily to develop and test their credentials under varying degrees of pressure. It's a way of supplementing both skill level and tournament income. Gambling is self-contained and doesn't pose any threat to the social player whether it's for the price of the table or higher stakes action. What can rouse the predator in a seasoned player, however, is a cocky novice: baseless bravado will always invite a lesson in pool and sometimes in humility.

Sharking is a technique used by some players to disrupt their opponent's concentration and confidence. Making noises or moving while a player is shooting are a few examples. If a player must resort to silly antics to gain an edge, it's a tipoff that he or she can't win by skill alone.

Hustling, unlike gambling, involves an act of deception. Some pool hustles, like cons, are elaborate schemes designed to reel in a sucker. Hustlers employ an insidious range of techniques, the most common of which is sandbagging – intentionally camouflaging their true skill level or *speed*.

The image of a predatory hustler is irresistible to mainstream media, as well as television and film producers. Understandably, this characterization is unpopular among competitive players, industry members and fans who live in the real billiard world. Well-managed billiard clubs, like golf courses, enforce good sportsmanship, decorum, discipline and a professional image.

 Remember: Win or lose, always *act* like a champion. Respect the equipment and your opponent.

POOLROOM ETIQUETTE
Do

✔ *Put the rack and rests back where they belong.* Searching for misplaced equipment wastes valuable playing time and can destroy your groove at the table.

✔ *Put house cues back in the rack after play.* Don't leave them standing up on an angle against the wall. This causes the wood to warp.

✔ *Retrieve the cue ball for your opponent if you've pocketed it or sent it flying off the table.*

✔ *Be a good sport.* Say "good game" before you break and – regardless of outcome – shake hands after a match.

✔ *Rack the balls properly for your opponent.* Ensure that the balls are frozen (touching) in the rack – particularly the first three.

✔ *Give up the table after you've missed!* Your turn is over. Sit down or stand well back, relax and relinquish your control.

✔ *Return a lost cue to management.* In many cases a player's cue has taken years to find and customize. Losing that cue can have a disastrous effect on a player's game and confidence.

Don't

✘ *Place a cigarette, cigar, glass or bottle on a pool table rail or cloth.*

✘ *Dump a tray or handful of balls on the table bed from a height.* This can chip the balls and the slate.

✘ *Take pool balls as souvenirs.* It aggravates the room owners – and players. The missing balls will be replaced but the result is a rack full of mismatched balls, which react poorly.

✘ *Put the chalk "dimple" or color-side down on the pool table rail.* This makes the rail dirty, which invariably transfers to everyone's hands and clothes.

✘ *Reach for the chalk when it's your opponent's turn to shoot.* You don't need to chalk after you've missed your shot. And if for some reason you do, carry your own cube and do it quietly and away from your opponent's space at the table.

✘ *Walk between a player and the table while he's surveying his next shot.* If you're carrying a tray of balls to your table, be conscious of matches in progress around you. Respect a player's space at the table: if you see that he's about to shoot, wait.

✘ *Stand in a player's line of aim or sight.* If, when your opponent is down on her shot, you can see her eyes – you should not be there. Move if you can. If it's too late and she's about to shoot, freeze.

✘ *Make any noise or movement during a player's shot.* Even if you're playing a social game, don't shoot the breeze while your opponent's shooting balls.

✘ *Say "great shot" repeatedly.* It's irritating and can upset a player's concentration. Say it afterwards or do what the pros do: pound the butt of your cue lightly on the ground three or four times in recognition.

✘ *Get terribly excited about a win you didn't earn.* If your opponent masterfully runs his balls, then loses by scratching on the 8-ball – and most of your balls are still on the table – pumping your fist in the air triumphantly is a little silly, isn't it?

5

Chapter Two

Equipment

A great player refines the art of pool.
Great equipment advances the science.

POOL CUES

While the one-piece **house cues** provided by your local pool club or bar are offered free of charge, most are well used and poorly maintained: some house cues are made from inferior wood and are badly warped. Loose ferrules and unplayable tips only add to the headache. If you want to achieve better results, regardless of your current ability, invest in your own cue and carrying case.

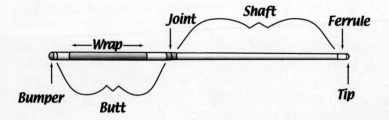

The two-piece jointed cue

A two-piece cue has a **shaft** and a **butt** that screw together at the joint. A well-made two-piece cue hits like it's one solid piece of wood but offers a big advantage: it can be easily transported in a cue case.

The majority of pool cue shafts are made of hard straight-grained maple. Butts are commonly crafted from hardwoods, such as bird's-eye maple, rosewood, ebony, cocobolo, morado and anjico and can feature a range of structural and decorative features. Graphite cues have become popular, as they're attractive and warp-resistant, but most players still prefer the character and *hit* of a wooden jointed cue.

You can get a respectable beginner or low-end cue for $50-150. Eventually, as your game develops, you may want to upgrade to a mid-range cue and keep your first cue to break the balls with. Mid-range and professional series cues offer better craftsmanship and longevity with better wood in the shaft, superior joints and more elaborate cosmetics in the butt.

Purchasing your own cue When purchasing a cue, you're looking for a special blend of balance, weight, length, taper and tip size: a cue that inspires you to play. How will you know if you've found the right cue? Hit a few balls. It feels a lot like love – you'll just know.

Technically, however, you should consider the following factors.

Cue balance This refers to how the weight of a cue is distributed. A poorly crafted cue might be back weighted or butt-heavy; the shaft will feel too light, as if it could float off your bridge hand.

Artificial weighting of cues is not recommended; naturally dense hardwoods provide the best feel – like the cue is an extension of your own arm. Playing with an unbalanced cue can force you to unconsciously compensate for the cue by moving your body and "steering" the shot, which is never a good thing.

The balance point in a well-crafted cue is approximately 45 to 47 cm (18 to19 in.) from the butt end of the cue.

Cue weight Pool cues range from 510 to 595 g (18 to 21 oz), 539 g (19 oz.) being the most popular choice.

Cue length   Pool cues are commonly 142.5 or 145 cm (57 or 58 in.) long. Some players prefer their cues to be 5 to 8 cm (2 to 3 in.) above their shoulders, others are content to have the tip reach their chest. Your height and the length of your limbs are determining factors: try an imaginary shot and let your backhand fall naturally to the proper cue grip. If you've got nothing to hold on to, you need a longer cue. If there's too much cue to handle, shorter is better.

Taper   The term taper describes the change in a cue shaft's diameter from the joint to the tip. This is an acquired preference that comes from hitting thousands of balls. A **straight taper** or **carom** is precisely that. If you lay the cue shaft down on a table, no light will pass underneath. A **pro tapered** shaft, starting from the tip and working toward the joint, gains one millimetre in diameter in the first 22 cm (9 in.) of shaft, with another millimeter gained in the next 12 cm (5 in.) down toward the joint.

Too radical a pro taper will produce a whippy cue: the narrow shaft flexes too much and you lose control of the cue ball. Too straight a taper and the result is a stiff hit; you want some flex for the proper application of draw, follow and English. The shaft's taper ultimately defines a cue's character.

Straightness   The best way to test for straightness in a two-piece cue is by rifle sighting. Hold the butt of the cue up to your eyes and look down the shaft. Rotate the cue as you're doing this and if there's a warp, you'll see it immediately. Rolling a two-piece cue on a table can hide minute flaws in the joint and shaft since the weight of the cue can hold the warp down.

Cue joints   The joint of a two-piece cue should approximate the feel and flex of a one-piece cue. Cues with aluminum joints are less expensive than wood or stainless steel. Stainless steel jointed cues are more costly and travel better, but none of these will make much of a difference to a beginner.

Joint protectors are two caps that screw on and into your joint when you're not using it. If you have a mid-range or professional series cues, joint protectors will keep the joint dry and protect it against any shock incurred during transportation.

Cue wrap   Irish linen or leather is comfortable, stylish and absorbent and ensures a non-slip grip when nervous wet palms are at play.

Bumper   The rubber stopper or plug found on the bottom of your cue has two main purposes. It allows you to rest the butt of your cue down on the floor while you're waiting for your opponent to miss. It also adds longevity: the bumper prevents the cue butt from cracking. Bumpers can become loose and fall out but are easily replaced.

Cue care

1.   Never leave your cue leaning up on an angle against a wall. This will cause it to warp, as will extreme heat or cold and moisture.
2.   A dirty pool cloth, humidity and nerves can make your hands and your cue sticky. Increase the slick factor by using a pool glove, a damp paper towel or a little talcum powder.
3.   Never sand your cue shaft. Use 1500 grade emory paper to clean it.
4.   Never break with your own playing cue. The break is a much harder shot; the shock can put your joint and tip at risk. If you don't have a break stick, use a house cue.

The **ferrule** is the connection between the tip and the cue shaft; it's your cue's shock absorber. Ferrules range in size according to preference and are made from either fiber or a more costly synthetic. Fiber is a paper-based product and considered by some players to be a natural extension of a wooden shaft.

Cue tips range in size from 12 to 14 mm, with 13 mm being the most popular tip size for players at all levels. A smaller tip will give you more sensitivity with the cue ball; to a beginner this may translate as a loss of control.

Cue tips are made of leather and rated on a scale from soft to hard. Generally, for a beginner, a softer tip provides the *feeling* of control: they compress more and remain on the cue ball longer.

However, they lose their shape from hit to hit and won't last as long as a hard tip. Additionally, as you begin to develop some snap in your stroke, you're bound to lose some control when spinning the cue ball. A harder tip will restore your command, plus you won't have to go through the trauma of breaking in a new tip as frequently.

A well-maintained tip is very important! As leather is hard, glazed and shiny by nature, you must roughen the surface slightly so that it can bond with chalk and stop costly miscues. For scuffing and shaping, use a commercial tip tool, a high-quality metal file or a small square of coarse sandpaper (200 grade or less). Scuffing doesn't mean sanding. Wiggle or press your tip into the scuffing device and loosen the fibers just enough to allow the tip to bond to the chalk.

Tips should be the same diameter as the cue, not bloated and hanging over the ferrule like a mushroom. They should also be domed, not flat or flush with the ferrule. Depending on how often you play (scuff and shape) and the quality of your tip, it will need replacing every three to 12 months. You can replace your own tips with a home repair kit, but it isn't advisable. Seek an expert: a cue mechanic or a player or pro in your local poolroom or billiard supply store.

THE POOL TABLE

Some people believe that pool table specifications should be standardized. Tables with tight pockets force players to be "on the money" to make a ball. Conversely, many believe that tables with "loose specs" are better for social players who want a less challenging table. To keep everybody happy, pool tables come in a broad assortment of models, materials, sizes and designs. Some conform to official specifications while others are designed to satisfy personal taste and decor. Some do both.

Pool tables consist of a frame (including four or six legs), table bed, six pockets and six cushions. The foot rail is where you rack the balls; the head rail is where you stand when you break.

Always twice as long as they are wide, pool tables range from 73 to 78 cm (29 to 31 in.) high. The standard size for coin-operated tables or "bar boxes" is 1.07 x ^{2}/₁₃ m (3½ x 7 ft.). The most popular

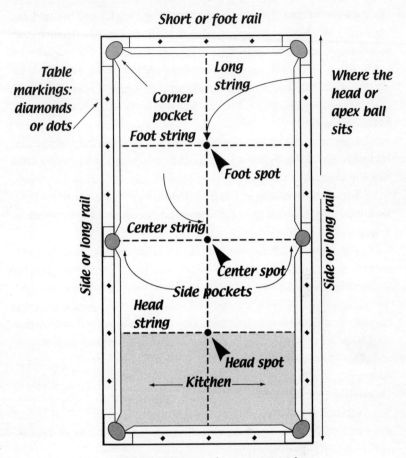

Short or foot rail

Table markings: diamonds or dots

Long string

Corner pocket

Foot string

Foot spot

Where the head or apex ball sits

Side or long rail

Center string

Center spot

Side pockets

Side or long rail

Head string

Head spot

Kitchen

Short or head rail: Your head is here when you lag and break

size for residential tables is 1.2 x 2.4 m (4 x 8 ft.). Commercial settings offer tables that are both 4 x 8 ft. for social players and 4½ x 9 ft. for tournament players.

To play pool enjoyably, a player requires at least one cue length (142.5 cm/57 in.) plus one backstroke (15-20 cm/6-8 in.) around each side to stand squarely at the table and draw his cue back without hitting any obstacles such as walls, pillars, furniture … or spectators.

Table beds   There's simply nothing like slate! This bed of rock offers weight, hardness and porosity, characteristics that are key to a smooth, stable, fast and durable playing surface.

The table bed of an eight- or nine- foot table consists of three pieces of slate that are sealed at the seams. Pool table slate ranges in thickness from 1 to 3 cm. The thicker the better and Italian slate is certainly the best!

Don't try and move your pool table without the help of a good table mechanic. Slate can come apart at the seams and render the bed unplayable.

Inexpensive home tables   If the only thing stopping you from buying your own pool table is money, keep reading! Here are a few ways to keep the cost down and the quality high.

For starters forget about that luxury table that's custom stained to match your other furniture. You don't really need sumptuous leather fringe pockets (or costly ball return pockets). Laminate legs are cheaper than hardwood, but very stable indeed. Fancy inlay in the rails and frame is nice, but unnecessary. And don't set your sights on 100 percent worsted wool cloth or Italian heated slate, either.

An all-dressed table will climb upward from a modest estimate of $3,500. If this is truly your heart's desire, perhaps it will help to know that most billiard retailers offer a financing plan. Some owners have secured bank loans: a pool table, like a car or a boat is an asset, after all, and as every good accountant knows, a pool table is a great way to entertain business clients.

For $2,000 to $3,000 you can get a well-playing, attractive home-use table. This price includes installation and accessories. Coin-operated tables range from $1,500 used to $3,500 new.

When selecting your table – new or used – don't scrimp on

A sturdy frame and legs. If you can budge a table with your body weight, don't waste your cash.

A slate table bed. For playability and durability you want a minimum thickness of 1.9 cm (3/4 in.).

Tight 80 percent wool, 20 percent nylon cloth. Not the most expensive nor the cheapest, but properly maintained, a middle line cloth should offer years of enjoyable play.

Pockets vary in size and cut and have highly technical measurements that can only excite table makers and installers. All a player really wants to know is, how wide is my gate? To check this, take two pool balls and fit them inside the mouth of the pocket. The mouth, also called the jaws, is the widest part of the pocket; it's the distance between the cushion tips or horns. If two balls fit snugly, then you'll need to be "on song" to sink a ball (the ideal practice table!). If there's a lot of room, the pockets are "buckets" – shoot out the lights!

The angle of the cushions is equally as important to a player. Simply put, fire a ball down the rail with your hand and watch what happens. If the ball drops without a wimper, it's a "clean fall." If a particular pocket argues with the ball (you see the ball rattling in the jaws before the pocket spits it out), be wary and use the information: play conservatively. Shoot slower. Play safe or play a different shot all together.

You can often find tables for sale in local newspapers. If you find one that has some meat on the frame and no visible flaws in the slate (gullies or shifted seams), but also has dead rails and a ripped cloth, consider this. A billiard mechanic can replace the cloth and rubber and level the table for $500, maybe less. Can you negotiate a price that will give you your dream table?

Pockets   There are two types of pockets on pool tables: drop and ball return. Most pocket billiard tables sport **drop pockets**. They're made of rubberized plastic or leather and have solid bottoms. **Ball return pockets** can be built into some table models but are commonly found on coin-operated or "bar box" tables. They have a hole in the bottom and are designed to direct pocketed balls through a system of troughs and into a ball return area.

Rails   Six **cushions**, also called rails, made of triangular rubber surround the table's playing surface. These pieces are actually equal in length; the long rails accommodate two cushions that are separated by a side pocket. Once the cushions have been glued to wooden rails, they're covered with billiard cloth and bolted down into the slate.

Before you play, it's advisable to check the condition of the cushions. Bolts can loosen, or the rubber can break away from the rail or lose its elasticity with age and become hard. "Dead" rails kill a ball's speed and spin and send it off at an improper angle, so if you have the choice, play on a different table. "Lively" rails are fast and make the rebound angle more acute.

To test the speed and health of the cushions, shoot the cue ball firmly into the foot or head rail. The cue ball should travel a few table lengths – without jumping. If the cue ball hops or appears to become trapped underneath the rail before bouncing off unpredictably, it's because the cushions have been fitted too low, or too high.

Cloth   The pool table bed, cushions and rails are covered in billiard cloth – not felt, as some people still call it. This fabric, made from a wool-nylon blend (worsted or non-worsted) comes in varying weights, weaves, colors, grades and prices. The composition, construction and finish of the cloth determine how smooth, consistent and durable it will be.

BALLS AND POOL ACCESSORIES

Pool balls come in different grades. Top tournament-quality pool balls are manufactured from a synthetic called phenolic resin and made to meet stricter standards for size, weight and balance. They're more expensive but the benefit is playability. Lower-grade and less expensive pool balls are suitable for most residential and commercial settings but may shrink or discolor at a faster rate than a high-quality set of balls.

A standard pool balls weighs 160 to 170 g (5½ to 6 oz.) and is 5.7 cm (2¼ in.) in diameter. In addition to an all-white cue ball, a standard set of pool balls includes 15 numbered balls: 1 to 7 are called "solids"; the 8-ball is black; 9 to15, "the stripes," are white with colored stripes around the middle. Some billiard stores carry new and very funky sets: clear, marbleized, pearlescent, sparkle, stars and stripes. These pool balls are guaranteed to add color and fun to your home game.

Pool accessories Every pool table should have extra equipment to assist you. The triangular-shaped **rack** allows you to tightly rack the balls for both full (15 ball) and partial (nine ball) rack games.

The **mechanical bridge** or rest or **rake** (forget the ancient phrase "ladies' helper") is found on hooks under the long rails. The rest acts like your bridge hand when you're shooting those hard-to-reach shots.

Cue cases are crafted to transport your cue and safeguard it from moisture and shock. Choosing a case can be almost as challenging as selecting your cue; you'll marvel at the craftsmanship and the wide range of design, color and size available in billiard supply stores and pro shops.

 Even if you're initially intending to take your cue no farther than the opposite end of your den, get an inexpensive hard case. Sheaths or soft padded cases don't offer the same protection against moisture and accidental shocks. Also, a case that features one or more zippered pockets is ideal for carrying useful tools (not to mention an extra pair of socks and a toothbrush for those long practice sessions).

Chapter Three

Cue control

If you devote the time now to developing a solid stance and a fluid stroke, you'll soon pass by a lot of experienced players who tried to run before they could walk. But to play pool really well, you'll need to develop an arsenal of shots ranging in speed, strength and character. Learn how to control your cue, and your options will be limitless.

THE BASIC STANCE

Your body is unique: your stance will be too. Common to all great players, however, is a stance that's solid, comfortable and balanced. Eventually you will just walk into your shot and fold over it naturally. But for now, keep this in mind: for you to pocket a ball, the cue must be delivered along a straight and precise path – the line of the shot. The secret to a great pool stance is to position your body around the cues, not the cue around your body. Take a few steps back. Clearly visualize the line of every shot *before* you get settled at the table. Let the line of the shot dictate your set-up at the table.

Also note that there will be many shots and conditions that require flexibility: to reach a cue ball you may have to lift one leg onto the table rail, or in tight playing quarters, practically perform yoga. In these cases, focus on keeping your bridge (the hand that supports and guides your cue shaft) steady, your body still and getting the cue through straight and unhindered.

Here's how to set up to take a shot. You can practice this at a pool table or even at home on your kitchen table.

The text book sample

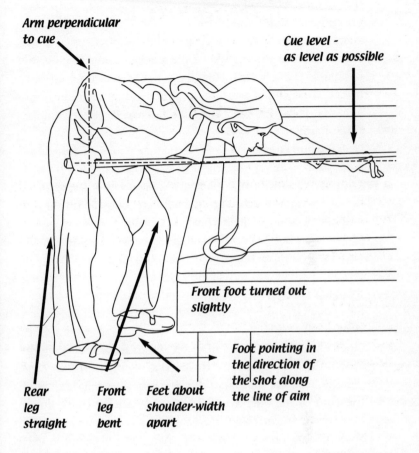

Arm perpendicular to cue

Cue level - as level as possible

Front foot turned out slightly

Foot pointing in the direction of the shot along the line of aim

Rear leg straight

Front leg bent

Feet about shoulder-width apart

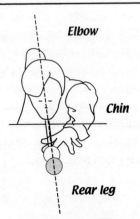

Elbow

Chin

Rear leg

Line of aim

1. Place the cue ball on the table. Select a pocket to play it into. (Position the cue ball so that you can comfortably place your bridge hand on the table.)

2. Stand back slightly for a clear view of the shot. Visualize a line that runs from the middle of the pocket back through the middle of the cue ball. This line would travel up your cue, bisect your chin (positioned directly over the cue) and continue back through your stroking arm. This is called the **line of aim**.

3. Grip the butt of your cue (right hand for righties, left for lefties) as if you were about to engage in a sword fight.

4. With you (and your hips) facing the direction of the shot, let the line of aim direct your cue. Balance your cue on the rail with the tip about an inch from the cue ball.

5. Secure your bridge hand under the cue shaft, about 15 to 20 cm (6 to 8 in.) from the cue ball.

6. Position your back foot (right for righties, left for lefties) along the line of aim. Your little toe should be lined up with the cue ball, pointing in the direction of the shot. *Lock this leg*; it stays rigid.

7. Open your other foot a comfortable distance (shoulders width) apart from your back foot. Turn it out slightly for balance. As you lean over the shot, *bend this leg*. Your hips will shift out of the path of the cue. Avoid the cowboy stance (both knees bent) or the spread eagle (legs too far apart).

8. Some players prefer to play with their chins grazing the cue; others have a more erect stance. If your vision is equal in both eyes, your chin should be centered directly over the line of the shot. Some players peer down the cue with their head slightly cocked to one side or the other. This is because one eye is stronger or dominant. Technically, it's not correct, but a lot of world-class players do it.

9. Your feet should be a comfortable distance back from the table. If your feet are too close, your stroke will feel cramped. If your feet are too far, your shot will be weak. Your momentum should be slightly forward, but not sinking into the slate.

10. Your body forms a tripod. Your weight should be evenly distributed between your bridge hand, right and left legs. Your head (chin), back foot, stroking arm (shoulder, forearm, tip of your elbow, wrist) should be on the same line as your cue and cue ball.

11. To test your stance, ask someone to give you a nudge. They shouldn't be able to budge you. When everything feels balanced, don't move. Relax. Take a few practice strokes. Let your muscles memorize the way this feels.

For a successful stroke

1. Watch great players but never copy another player's stance. Spend some solitary time getting to know your body at the table.

2. Use mirrors, video cameras and seasoned players (who can teach) to evaluate your cueing action.

3. Learn to hit the cue ball correctly before practicing with an object ball.

BRIDGES

The first thing you commit to the table when you set up for a shot is your bridge - the hand that slides under your cue shaft, typically 15 to 20 cm (6 to 8 in.) from the cue ball. The purpose of your bridge is to support and guide your cue shaft throughout its delivery. If it's weak or unsteady, your bridge will lend instability to your entire stance and stroke.

Some players bend or crook their bridge arm, which means that both their hand and forearm are on the cloth and their heads are lower to the playing surface. Other players prefer a straight bridge arm; this stops their bodies from lurching forward with the shot, especially when under pressure. There should be a little tension in your bridge arm; it helps keep your body still while shooting and frees up your stroking arm.

There are several styles of bridges. When you're shooting a shot where you have room to place your hand on the table, you will use a **basic bridge**. You will either cup your hand on the cloth and make an **open bridge**, or form a loop with your thumb and first finger and make a **closed bridge**. The open bridge offers one quick advantage: it's easy to form. Some players use an open bridge for below center hits on the cue ball and then switch to a closed bridge for touch, finesse, topspin or power shots. There are players who are grateful for the confinement of the closed bridge: they no longer finish shots with their cues in the air. Let the shot dictate which bridge is best.

You will also have to adapt your basic bridge to other circumstances such as shots where the cue ball is frozen to the cushion, or touching an obstructing ball. In these instances, it helps to shorten your stroke (the length of your backswing) and stay still. Don't be afraid to alter your stance for increased balance. And for heaven's sake, chalk up!

The open bridge

Raise and lower your knuckles for middle, low and high-ball shots

The loop bridge

Open, snooker or V-bridge

1. Place your hand on the table bed and spread your fingers as wide as possible. Raise your knuckles only.
2. Cock your thumb up and press it against the side of your index finger. Together your cocked thumb and index finger form a V or a groove over which the cue can travel. Never separate these two fingers as the cue will roll around in the gap and ruin your accuracy.
3. The pads of your fingers and heel of your hand are positioned solidly on the cloth
4. Your middle, ring and little finger should be spread (comfortably) for balance

Loop bridges

1. Make a fist with your bridge hand.
2. Slide the cue under your index finger.
3. Press the tip of your index finger against the tip of your thumb to form a loop.
4. Stretch out your middle, ring and little fingers.
5. Spread your ring and little finger out for balance.

 If you're used to playing with a weak bridge, at first the sensation of splaying your little, ring and middle fingers and gripping the cloth may feel uncomfortable. This too will pass! Train the muscles in your hand to form a balanced bridge.

Basic bridge for middle ball, low ball and high ball shots

To hit a standard below-center shot, you can't just lift the butt of your cue and jab down at the cue ball, or when applying topspin, lower the butt and poke up at the ball. Your cue must be as level as possible through the delivery. To accomplish this, don't raise or lower your elbow – raise or lower your bridge hand.

For middle or high ball shots, cup your hand and raise your knuckles. This elevates your bridge (and your cue shaft) to the level you want your tip to contact the cue ball. Even though your knuckles are raised, your fingertips and the heel of your hand must remain on the cloth for stability. (Don't bend your fingers at the joints.) Now, check the butt of your cue. Is it level? If not, drop it. When striking low ball, lower your knuckles and form a flatter bridge

Rail bridges *When the cue ball is a few inches from the cushion,* you must form your bridge on the rail to shoot. For this you will use a variation of the open bridge. Place your hand on the rail. Tuck your thumb under your middle finger. Slide your cue under your first finger and guide your cue against the inside of your middle finger.

If the cue ball is frozen to the cushion, and you can only see the top of the ball, your best bet is to use an open bridge. Lay your hand on the edge of the rail, gripping it with your fingertips. Drop your wrist and concentrate on pressing the cue down to keep it level through your stroke.

To hit below center on a cue ball near the cushion, form an open bridge but elevate it slightly: lift the heel of your hand so that your bridge is balanced on the rail on the first joints of all four fingers. Your thumb is cocked and pressed against your first finger. Elevate the butt of your cue and, with a short stroke, strike down on the cue ball, hitting as close to the middle as you can. You may have to circle your front leg around to the side and assume a sideways stance to accommodate the elevated cue stick.

The elevated bridge when shooting over a blocking ball

Bridging over a ball   When the cue ball is touching another ball, you must bridge over it and shoot away from the intervening ball. The closer the intervening ball is to the cue ball, the greater your cue must be elevated.

To form this bridge, spread and press the tips of your little, ring and middle finger into the cloth behind the intervening ball. Your first and middle fingers are in front and your little finger behind. (Your first finger should be about an inch from the intervening ball.) Cock your thumb up high and press it against your first finger, which drops comfortably behind your middle finger; the first finger balances the little finger and adds support to this otherwise flimsy bridge.

Mechanical bridge stance   When you've run out of torso and can't get your bridge hand close enough to the cue ball, get the mechanical bridge. Space permitting, place the bridge on the table at an angle to the line of aim. If you're right-handed, anchor it by placing your left hand over the handle.

The mechanical bridge stance

Keep your elbow up

Grip the butt of your cue with your thumb underneath and your other fingers on top for support. Place your cue on the bridge head, ensuring that you have 15 to 20 cm (6 to 8 in.) of shaft in front. The bridge head has three different notches or grooves. Place your cue in the higher notch (in the middle) for follow or center ball shots, and in the lower notches (outside right and left) for stun or draw shots. Your elbow should be pointing out to the side, with your forearm parallel with the table. Reverse your stance: bend your back leg and keep the other braced – and on the line of the shot.

If you must hold the bridge up in your hand, or bridge over another ball, take a few preliminary strokes. Don't release the cue until you're balanced and calm. As the butt of your cue will be elevated, chalk up and try not to dig at the cue ball. Shorten your backstroke for more control and *punch* the shot.

THE GRIP

Lay your cue down on the table and pick it up. That's your natural grip: firm, but not rigid (no fingertips, please). Your thumb and index finger are actually holding the cue while the other fingers add balance and keep the cue on a straight line.

In *The Book of Five Rings* on how to hold the long sword, Musashi wrote, "Rigidity means a dead hand and flexibility means a living hand. "The same thing applies to gripping a pool cue. Your grip hand *pumps* the life into a great stroke.

The grip

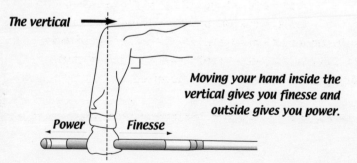

The vertical ➤

Moving your hand inside the vertical gives you finesse and outside gives you power.

◄ Power   Finesse ►

Ideally, you will want to grip the cue around 20 to 25 cm (8 to 10 in.) from the bumper. But this doesn't take into consideration players with long arms and short cues. Let your hand grip the butt so that your forearm is perpendicular, and don't forget to check that your knuckles are in a straight line with your forearm and the floor – not twisted in or out.

The line that runs through your forearm, forming a right angle with your cue is called the **vertical**. For a soft hit you may want to **shorten the cue** by moving your hand inside the vertical, closer to the joint. On a power shot that requires more backstroke and/or a longer follow-through, slide your hand outside the vertical and closer to the bumper. But be careful: the more "loose" cue you have, the more accuracy you'll need to keep the cue on a straight line.

At the moment that your tip strikes the cue ball, on most shots, your forearm should be perpendicular with the cue. You don't want to be inside or outside the vertical. Women players who find that their bodies are interfering with the normal delivery of the cue, may want to try sliding their grip hand a bit outside the vertical. This way the tip of your cue will reach the cue ball before your wrist can contact your upper body.

Shooting over another ball with the mechanical bridge

A pool bridge head will flip over to its side to form a taller bridge. But occasionally pool tables are fitted with snooker or X-head rests, which aren't designed to do this. In this case, you can still shoot over a ball by carefully fitting a second mechanical bridge on top.

THE PENDULUM STROKE

Once you have learned how to setup properly at the pool table, you can begin concentrating on your cueing action or stroke. For a fluent and straight stroke, think of your elbow as a hinge that swings the cue to and fro, like a pendulum.

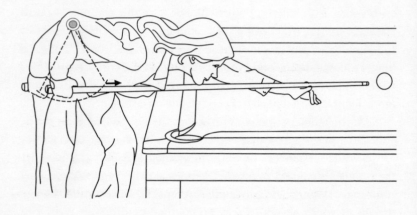

Your elbow and forearm draw back the cue slowly. You pause, then propel the cue forward smoothly. Your elbow, forearm, wrist and cue move. The rest of your body remains still; excess body movement promotes an imprecise hit. Don't muscle or poke the ball, stroke it: let the cue do the work.

The stroke can be broken down into five separate stages:

1. **Warm-up or feather strokes** Before executing your shot, always take a few preliminary strokes to check your alignment and harness your focus. This is called feathering the cue ball. Bring the tip of your cue up to the cue ball so that it almost touches and draw it back, and repeat, maintaining a consistent rhythm.

2. **Backstroke** Let your elbow and forearm draw back the cue: think slow, level and straight. Learn to control your cue on the way back. If you take the cue back on an angle, it won't come through straight. Also, the longer the backstroke, the more cue you'll have to control on the delivery. When some players have

trouble with their stroke, they shorten their backstroke until their "groove" reappears.

3. **Pause** Some players start their stroke with the tip of their cue a breath away from the cue ball; they begin their backstroke and release the cue immediately. Others prefer the pause at the end of their backstroke; they pull the cue back slowly, pause, and then pull the trigger. Find out what works best for you.

4. **Hit** How the tip of your cue strikes the cue ball determines the quality of the hit. A clean or "sweet" hit hinges on the fluid coordination of all of the stages of a stroke.

5. **Follow through or finish** There's a saying in the poolroom: hit the ball, Alice! The idea is that you should never tap, baby or jab at the cue ball – you must accelerate *through* the cue ball.

When shooting, keep your head down until your cue has come to a natural stop. Don't pop up prematurely (either a split-second before or during your follow-through) to see if you've pocketed your object ball. If your head is coming up, so is the cue; and no good can come from this!

To cure this bad habit, try exaggerating the length of time you stay down on a few shots. Force yourself to relax. Let the cue go and don't move until the cue ball comes to a full stop.

Chapter Four

Cue ball control

While learning to control your cue - stance and stroke - your primary concern was the path of the cue ball to the object ball. Cue ball control is the study of the paths of the cue ball before and *after* contact with the object ball and cushions.

The more you play, the more you'll discover that there are variables and shifting relationships affecting the way the cue ball behaves. Not all of these can be addressed in a book. It comes from experience. From here on in, you really have to hit balls - the same shot over and over again. Keep the speed constant, but experiment with the angle and fullness of contact; alter the speed; try different degrees of spin; change the distance between the object ball and the cue ball; shoot on different tables.

The challenge and combinations are infinite. Yet, one thing remains certain: the outcome of any shot is wholly dependent on how well you hit it. Befriend the cue ball and the game begins to reveal its coveted secrets.

CHALK UP!

Centuries ago, players tried to prevent their cues from sliding off the cue ball by coating their tips with sidewalk chalk, or simply by twisting their cues into plaster ceilings and walls. It didn't work then, so don't do it today. Ordinary chalk is carbonate of lime, a light powdery substance that's ideal for writing pool scores on a blackboard, but it won't foil a foul stroke or allow you to spin a ball.

Billiards chalk (still called *chalk*) is an entirely different compound. It's made from pigment, binder and silica. The key ingredient is silica, an abrasive that creates the friction necessary for a hard, slick tip to grip the round polished surface of a cue ball.

A **miscue** is an improperly executed stroke caused by poor contact between your tip and the cue ball. This can cause the balls to veer off unpredictably. You must apply chalk to your cue tip on every shot or every second shot to prevent costly miscues.

Apply a thin, even coating of chalk to your tip every shot if you can. If there's still a bald spot, cover it up with light, feathery strokes. If the tip feels like it's rejecting the chalk, examine it. Is it hard or glazed? If so it will need to be roughened up or scuffed before it will accept chalk.

Never cake chalk on. Too much chalk will leave a deposit on the cue ball. If there's a dollop of chalk on the exact point where the two balls meet on impact, you'll get a **kick** (a slight jump or hiccup in the object ball that alters its path and speed) or a **skid**.

Don't jam your tip into the chalk and grind a hole through the center. This chalks your ferrule, not your cue tip. Hold the chalk in one hand. Grip the top of your cue with the other. Turn your cue slowly while the other hand glides the chalk across the tip. Now you're ready to rack 'n' roll!

BASIC AIM TRAINING

Straight-in shots versus angles   Set up a shot where the cue ball, the **object ball** (the ball you want to pocket) and the pocket are in a straight line. Hitting the cue ball in the center, aim the cue ball straight at the object ball to contact it full in the face. This is a **straight-in** shot. If you miss this shot, then your aim isn't the only problem. Review the last chapter on stance and stroke!

If the cue ball, object ball and pocket are not all lined up, then your shot involves hitting the object ball at an angle or cutting the ball in.

The line of aim, point of impact and point of aim   In a nutshell: to pocket an object ball you must shoot the cue ball at a target (**point of aim**) so that it travels along a path (**line of aim**) to hit a point on the object ball (**point of impact**).

Certain shots, such as a fine cut shot, are more difficult as the point of impact is a specific point. The cue ball must collide with the object ball at this precise point or it's "good night, Irene!" Others will offer a larger target area and thus a greater margin for error. For example, if a ball is sitting right over the pocket, you have a larger target area: the cue ball can hit one of a few different points around its middle and still sink it. The following exercise will help clarify the heady aspect of aim.

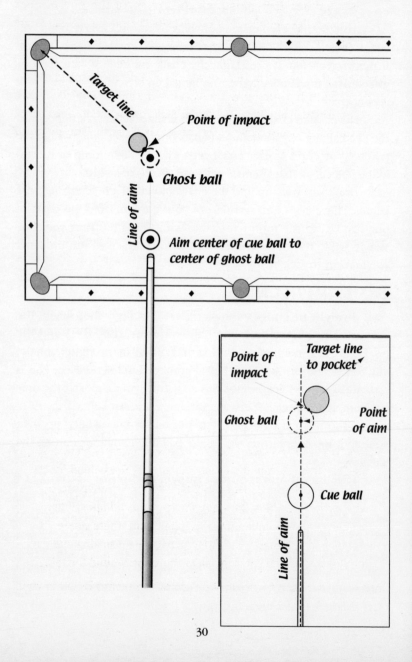

1. Set up the cue ball (not too close to the pocket) and an object ball at an angle.
2. Visualize an imaginary line that runs from the center of the cue ball through the center of the object ball. Now establish a second line that runs from the center of the pocket back through the middle of the object ball. Find the point where these two lines intersect. This is the **point of impact**. The cue ball must contact the object ball at this point to pocket it.
3. Aim the cue ball at this specific point, and the result is a thick hit and (depending on the distances) a miss. Why? Pool balls are round. They have big fat bellies. To pocket an object ball, you have to aim to allow for the cue ball's girth. **The point of aim is *not* the point of impact.**
4. How do you find the point of aim? To determine this, imagine or physically place (in practice only) a third ball behind the object ball so that it touches the point of impact. A line of centers drawn through these two balls points into the back of the pocket. This third ball is called a **ghost ball**. It's where your cue ball must be at the moment of impact to pocket the object ball. The **point of aim** is found at the center of the ghost ball.
5. Visualizing this ghost ball will help you shoot more accurately: **just aim the center of the cue ball through the center of the ghost ball.**
6. The **line of aim** runs from the center of the cue ball to the center of the ghost ball.

When assessing your shots, take a few steps back from the table. You'll have a much clearer picture of the relevant distances and angles. Get behind the pocket in question and take a look. If you're faced with a cut shot where the steep angle makes it impossible to see the contact point on the object ball from where you're standing, don't guess. The difference between sinking and missing a long fine cut is usually a short jog around the table.

Sighting   When aiming, your eyes can dart back and forth between the cue ball, object ball and the pocket; but when you pull the trigger, lock your eyes on the object ball. Many players who pause briefly at the end of their backstroke use this moment to switch their eyes onto the object ball.

Center pocket   While there are many measurements that will affect the way a pocket accepts or rejects pool balls, when aiming you should be concerned with two things: opening and cut.

Technically, the pocket opening (or jaws) is the distance between the two cushion points or tips. A common mistake is to think that pocket center is always in the middle of this opening – and as a result routinely aim to send your object ball into the back of the pocket. On a straight-in shot (a ball on the foot spot that's being shot into the corner pocket), this is true. But move the object ball closer to the short or side rails and suddenly one side of the pocket, because of the tip, closes up, and the other, because of the inside face of the cushion, opens up. Your target area – and hence, pocket center – *shifts*. On shots like these, you'll rob yourself of a much larger target if you're aiming at the back of the pocket.

Also, unlike snooker, all pool pockets are not cut from a standardized template so pocket anatomies vary from table to table. Rounded jaws are small, stingy and rude: when playing down the cushion they'll spit your ball back at you. Inside siding helps (refer to Chapter 4). If the pockets are square-cut, you'll have a more generous target area: this cushion face smiles favorably on well-aimed balls.

Cheating the pocket   Remember, pool pockets are large enough to position two pool balls side by side at the mouth. And that's a tight pocket; many pockets are wider still. This means that you don't have to shoot every shot into the center or heart of the pocket. Depending on the angle of the shot, if you aim to cheat or direct the object ball to either side of the pocket, you've also altered the path of the cue ball after contact. Cheating the pocket is a wonderful way to position the cue ball without having to use anything riskier than a plain ball hit.

SPEED: SOFT, HARD AND HAPPY MEDIUM HITS

Beginners tend to hit most of their balls with either too much force, or little. A versatile range of cue speeds easily distinguishes a skilled player. Let your muscles begin memorizing the following hits:

- Place the cue ball on the head spot and hit it one table length (over the spots) to just reach the center of the foot rail. This is a **soft hit**.
- Now hit the ball two table lengths (until the cue ball returns to the head rail). This is a **medium hit**. Get comfortable with this hit, as a lot of your shots will be executed at roughly this speed.
- Finally, control the cue and power the ball at least three table lengths (head spot, foot rail, head rail). This is a **hard hit**. If your cue ball stayed more or less on the long string and across the spots the entire time, congratulations. You're in dead stroke!

You will come to appreciate that the terms soft, medium and hard are relative. Every player has a different stroke: the amount of force transferred to the cue ball will ultimately depend on how well you hit it.

More about soft

- Remember that a soft hit is still a *hit* – don't treat the cue ball like an egg. Reduce your cue speed but don't be afraid to go *through* the white ball.
- The softer a ball is hit, the more susceptible it is to any flaw in the table or cloth. If one side or area of the table gives you grief, try a harder hit.
- Some pockets have a speed limit: hit a ball too fast and the pocket won't accept it. You'll have to learn to play **pocket speed** on certain tables.

More about hard

- Only hit a ball hard if there is no other way to play the shot. If you have a flair for the dramatic, try acting – not pool.
- The harder the hit, the more cue control you'll need.
- You'll get more power by a longer backstroke; a longer

follow-through; moving your hand back along the grip of your cue; and increased but carefully controlled acceleration through the cue ball.

- Never rush your backstroke. An effective power shot is only possible with a fluid stroke and controlled acceleration through the cue ball.

Cue ball to object ball contact   The following illustration outlines the general range of cue ball to object ball contacts from a straight-in shot (full cue ball to object ball) to a fine cut shot (edge to edge).

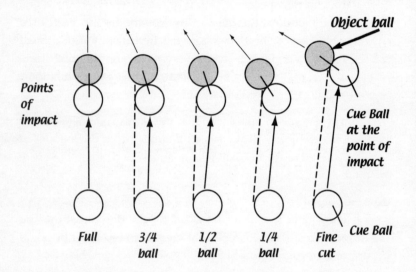

Speed transfer: thick and thin hits   By altering the fullness of the contact, you can sink your object ball and, after contact, get the cue ball to a few different spots on the table. On some shots, this is a great way to position the cue ball for your next shot using a low-risk center ball hit.

If the cue ball contacts the object ball full in the face, it transfers a great deal of its energy to the object ball. This cue ball runs out of juice and will not go far after contact unless you increase your cue speed. Billiards players call full contact hits **driving** the ball.

Conversely, increase the angle of the shot by hitting the object ball thinner (at the same speed), and watch *whitey* go! The cue ball has the energy to travel the table. This is called **cutting** the ball.

Pool players often refer to the cue ball affectionately as "whitey" or the "rock."

THE TRAVELS AND TRAVAILS OF THE CUE BALL

Where your tip strikes the cue ball determines the direction of the object ball and the path that the cue ball will take after contact. Striking the cue ball precisely in the middle is also referred to as a center or plain ball hit because it doesn't curve or reverse. It slides first, then rolls and rebounds off the cushion *naturally*. To play billiards well, you must first *master* the art of a precise and consistent center ball hit.

The minute you start striking the cue ball high, low, right or left of center and vary the cue speed and force – *whitey* takes off on a series of adventures that deviate from this natural path. You won't be able to predict or control this behavior without a basic grasp of the way a plain ball likes to react.

There are many ways to position a cue ball to the same spot on the table. You can often get the cue ball to position X with a center ball hit by altering speed or aim. But on certain shots, this will be impossible. Now you're forced to alter the natural path of the cue ball and that involves executing a non-center ball hit. A versatile arsenal of center and non-center ball hits is crucial for positional play, breaking up clusters of balls and avoiding scratches.

Center ball   When you hit **center** cue ball at **medium** speed, the cue ball glances off the object ball along a path called the tangent or right angle line. To calculate this key path:

1.   Visualize a ghost ball behind the object ball. Let your mind's eye establish a line that runs through the middle of both balls

to pocket center. Call this line the **target line**. This is the path that the object ball will take on its way to the pocket.

2. Through the point of impact (between the object and ghost balls) draw another line that bisects the target line at a right angle (90°). Call this the **tangent** or **right angle line**. This represents the natural path that the cue ball will take after contact with the object ball – on a center ball hit. The angle at which this cue ball then approaches the cushion (angle of incidence) *should* equal the angle of rebound.

Wherever possible, position the cue ball with a plain ball hit. Striking the cue ball in the center lowers the risk of miscues and variables such as deflection and throw that will only complicate your early results and increase your chance of missing. Most cue balls are marked with a red dot, which can be positioned into place and used as a guide during practice. Refer to the drills in Chapter 10.

Slide versus roll When you shoot a center ball shot at medium speed, the cue ball will actually slide forward for a few inches before it begins to revolve. It's the friction in the cloth that stimulates the forward roll.

You can turn a slide into a roll over a short distance by shooting the cue ball softly.

Friction will also turn a slide into a forward spin at longer distances. This may not mean much to you in the early stages, but it will come in handy when you start playing a shot with stun or stop action.

Follow If you cut an object ball at medium speed using a tip's worth (above center) of follow or topspin, the following drama ensues: the cue ball collides with the object ball and sends it off toward the pocket. Upon contact the cue ball shimmies along the 90° tangent line. It stops for a moment to say "hey, wait up", curves away from the plain ball path, then zooms forward, hell-bent to follow forward.

After contact, the shape of the forward curve is determined by how hard you drive the cue ball. The harder the hit, the longer it takes the cue ball to curve, and the greater the distance that the cue ball travels along the tangent line before bending forward. A soft hit produces a sharp curve. A hard hit flattens this initial curve and sends the cue ball farther along the tangent line before it bends forward.

Striking the cue ball a half to a full tip above center will give you a sufficient amount of follow. Naturally, the higher your tip strikes on the cue ball, the more topspin you'll apply. Speed, the position and distance between balls and the fullness of the hit will all affect the actual path and the distance that your cue ball will follow after contact.

If you hit a follow shot really high and hard, this is called force follow. When an incredibly energetic cue ball drives an object ball into a pocket, then meets resistance upon impact (a springy cushion), the result is amazing: *whitey* gets "lazy." With a little control and practice, this shot can be used to kill the cue ball's speed rebounding off a cushion.

Stop, stun and stun follow   Striking the cue ball marginally below center gives you these critical shots. On a full, *straight-in* contact imparting a slight amount of reverse spin – at a certain distance – this will **stop** the cue ball dead in its tracks. On an *angle*, the same stroke will **stun** the cue ball's action after contact. These are versatile shots with great positional benefits: stop and stun shots allow you to keep the cue ball on a very short tether.

The deadball and straight-in stop shots   On a straight-in shot, if your cue ball and object ball are close enough together (15 cm / 6 in.) the cue ball doesn't have very much distance to grab quality friction from the cloth. So, still sliding – not rolling or spinning – when it contacts the middle of the object ball, it gives all of its life force to the object ball instantly and stops dead, ironically enough occupying the exact same position as the ghost ball. This reaction is dependent on a precise center cue ball to *center* object ball contact and a reasonable pace. If the centers aren't meeting, the cue ball will drift off sideways; a soft hit arouses friction in the cloth, which then turns the slide to a forward roll.

Now, move the cue ball and the object ball a little farther apart and shoot this straight-in shot. The friction in the cloth begins to convert the gentle slide into a rollicking roll. Upon contact, on a plain ball hit at the same speed, the cue ball will roll forward after contact. So, in order to make the cue ball stop dead now, you must strike the cue ball slightly below center to add a marginal amount of reverse spin. The cue ball will not stop dead unless it's carrying reverse spin at the moment of impact. The greater the distance between the cue ball and the object ball, the more reverse spin you'll need to apply to the cue ball. This effect is achieved by hitting the cue ball lower and, in some instances, increasing cue speed.

On straight-in shots, at certain distances (which will vary from table to table) center ball stop shots (as opposed to mild draw) are possible if a hard stroke is used, as a hard hit prolongs the slide stage. This tends to be a more risky enterprise: it's always harder to control your stroking arm when adrenaline is surging than to accurately position your tip lower on the cue ball.

The stun shot   Stop and stun are twin shots: fraternal not identical. On a straight-in shot, stop action stops the cue ball dead. On a cut or angle shot, however, using the same stroke, because of the thinner contact, the cue ball is still registering vital signs after impact. The stop action stuns the cue ball, and it departs sideways (albeit slowly) along the right-angle tangent line. Stunning a ball reduces the cue ball's run after glancing off the object ball. The angle determines just how much stun action will be transferred to the cue ball.

The stun follow shot   If you shoot a short-distance center ball shot softly or a hard long shot, the friction of the cloth will turn slide into a forward roll. Your plain ball stop shot suddenly translates into a follow shot. You can now use this to your advantage. If you need to position your cue ball a few inches to a foot past the object ball for your next shot, hit it with stun follow.

Draw   When the cue ball, object ball and pocket are in a straight line, if you hit middle cue ball a tip's width below center you propel the object ball forward toward the pocket and the cue ball should come straight back toward you. (What, you say? Sometimes my cue ball stops dead instead of reversing? Or, even more aggravating, it rolls forward and follows the object ball into the pocket?) If this is happening, there's a perfectly good reason: your cue ball will not draw back without reverse spin.

After the cue ball has left the tip of your cue, it slides briefly before revolving backward, bottom over top, in a reverse spin. Friction causes this reverse spin to eventually run out, at which point the ball keeps sliding before coming to a full top-over-bottom *roll*. If your cue ball contacts the object ball before or after it's spinning in reverse (while sliding or rolling) – well then, your draw shot's a bust.

For this and many reasons, a good draw shot is harder to control than follow. Practice will give you a more confident command of this beautiful shot, and give you a feel for the way that distance, speed and *timing* of the hit can affect your results.

Draw is easier on balls that are closer together, as the cue ball will contact the object ball while it's got plenty of reverse spin. Decrease that distance and you're facing a nip shot that requires intestinal fortitude and sound reflexes. (You'll need to pull the cue away in good time.) Increase this distance significantly, and on a basic (a tip below center) draw shot, the reverse spin is either dead or dying. On these shots you must often hit the cue ball lower and harder with an extreme or power draw, which gives you a faster reverse spin. Also, the harder you hit the cue ball, the longer the reverse spin stays on the cue ball.

The paths the cue ball will take after contact with center, high and low ball hits

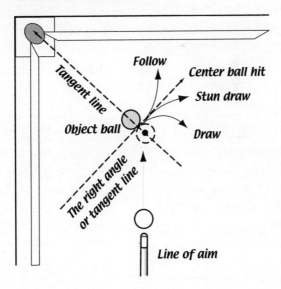

Proper English   English is used when you can't get the cue ball to a specific spot on the table any other way. If you've mastered the center and non-center hits that run along the vertical axis of the cue ball, you can now begin to experiment hitting the cue ball to the left and right of center. Combine this with a stroke and this will give you proper English.

Start by practicing, with a striped ball as your cue ball. Strike the cue ball slowly and deliberately a tip to the right of center and watch *whitey* stray brazenly off-line. Now with the cue ball and object ball a few feet apart, try to pocket a few balls. Your aim could be 100 percent true – but you might miss the pocket, perhaps even the object ball, by a mystifying measure. Don't fret: you're not alone. Spinning a ball can sometimes make a seasoned player feel like Alice playing pool in Wonderland.

Using proper English – in a sentence

It's helpful and equally confounding to learn that English has a language of its own. Left and right English is called "spin," (despite follow being topspin and draw being reverse spin). It's also referred to as right or left siding. What can get tricky for some players are the qualifiers **running** and **check,** as well as **inside** and **outside siding.**

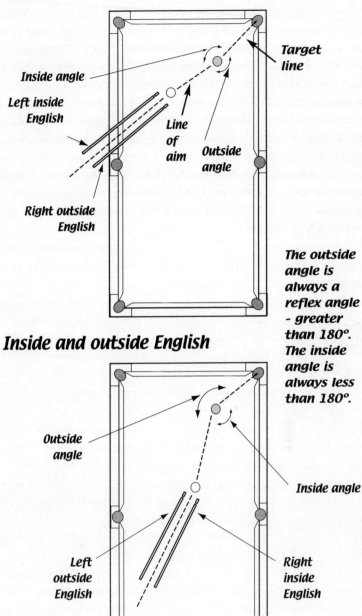

Inside angle

Target line

Left inside English

Line of aim

Outside angle

Right outside English

The outside angle is always a reflex angle - greater than 180°. The inside angle is always less than 180°.

Inside and outside English

Outside angle

Inside angle

Left outside English

Right inside English

On every shot an angle is formed between the line of aim (cue ball to the object ball) and the target line (object ball to the pocket). If the tip of your cue is addressing the right edge of a cue ball that's adjacent to the outside angle of the shot, then you're applying right outside English. Now on this same shot, if the tip of your cue is addressing the left edge of the cue ball (which is now facing the inside angle), you can say that you're about to use left inside English.

Is your head spinning? Good. It's time to impart some of that to the cue ball – if and only if you've got the stroke, or all that you'll be spinning here is your wheels!

Deflection and throw: hitting, and missing, with English Applying sidespin to the cue ball alters the cue ball's path to the object ball. This increases your margin of error – dramatically. Right English causes the cue ball to revolve counter-clockwise. The cue ball then pushes out to the left (called **deflection** or **squirt**) before eventually curving back to the right and across the line of aim. Left English gives the opposite reaction.

Now, it's difficult enough having to predict the character of a curve *after* contact (as in a follow or draw shot). But, should the cue ball stray, at least you've already pocketed your object ball. With spin, however, if the cue ball contacts the object ball at the wrong stage of the curve, it's a dog's breakfast!

Another factor affecting spin is **throw**. When a cue ball hit with English makes contact with an object ball, it throws the object ball marginally off the target line. On occasion this variable will help you pocket a ball that you thought was the impossible dream. It can also make you miss balls that you thought were a birthday present.

The degree of spin, speed and distance will affect the curve of the cue ball travelling to the object ball. The farther your tip strikes towards the edge of the cue ball, the more siding you'll get. Also, the softer the hit, the more spin you'll impart to the cue ball. The more siding, the farther the cue ball will curve off the line of aim on its way to the cue ball. The greater the distance between the cue ball and the object ball, the easier it is to miss the object ball completely.

Applying English To apply right English, set up your bridge hand and stance so that your tip and cue are going through the right side of the cue ball in a straight line to a point beyond the cushion.

(One-half to a full tip's width to the right or the left of center is generally enough.) Some pool players set up for a center ball hit and stroke across the cue ball to strike the right or left side. This approach lessens deflection but makes aiming much more difficult.

In summary, spin alters the path of the cue ball to the object ball. Upon contact, the cue ball glances off the object ball normally. *After* contact is when the effect of sidespin is the most pronounced.

Using right-hand English, shoot the cue ball slowly towards the center diamond of the opposite rail. The cue ball is revolving to the left, but watch the cue ball contact the cushion and return to the right. Left English will have the opposite effect.

What actually happens when a ball, hit with right English, contacts the object ball? The right English transfers (a little) left English to the object ball and the object ball is thrown to the left. (The exact opposite happens with left English.) You must take this into consideration when aiming, and adjust the thickness of your hit accordingly.

Running siding increases the speed of the cue ball after contact so that it travels faster and farther: the cue ball literally runs off the rail. It will widen the angle of rebound or lengthen the shot off the cushion. **Check siding** kills the cue ball's speed after contact and minimizes the cue ball's run. At the same speed this effect narrows the angle of rebound or shortens the shot off the cushion. The thinner the cut, the more difficult it is to check the ball. A hard hit will minimize throw; a soft hit amplifies this variable.

As a handy rule, follow, stun and draw shots will not alter the natural path of the cue ball to the object ball. Spin shots – left and right English – will. Follow, stun and draw shots change the natural path of the cue ball after contact with the object ball. Spin shots – left and right English – (at the same speed) do not alter the natural path of the cue ball after contact with the object ball but do alter that path after contact with a cushion.

Chapter Five

The break and other critical shots

The break and other critical shots are the building blocks of a competitive pool game. Some of these shots will show up time and time again. Others are well hidden: diamonds in the rough once you know how to play them. Learn these challenging shots, and you'll soon have an arsenal of game winners.

BREAK SHOT

The crush. The bust. The snap. No matter what you call it, the break is one of the most important shots in pool. There are two key things to remember about the break:

1. Given the choice, take it. It's a big advantage, in every game except straight pool. Practice this critical shot diligently. Many games are won and lost from the break.
2. As with any pool shot, your goal is to position the cue ball after contact.

There are two kinds of breaks: open and safe. The **open break** is an offensive shot. It's executed in games such as 8-ball and 9-ball where you want to drop some balls, bust up the pack and leave the cue ball resting in middle of the table where you have a choice of many shots.

The **safe break** is a defensive shot. It's used in games such as straight pool, or one pocket, where the opening strategy is to position the cue ball in a spot (near or on the head rail) that gives your opponent either no object ball to pocket or a very difficult shot at that. Eventually one defender will lose control of this opening safety exchange and the other will gladly assume the role of attacker.

One thing common to the break in all pool games is the importance of a proper **rack.** Check to see whether the rack is tight. If it's not, ask your opponent to rerack, ensuring that the head or apex (first) ball and as many of the other balls are frozen (touching) as possible. A loose or "gaff" rack will undermine the finesse or force of a great break shot. Also ensure the rack is properly aligned. The back row of balls should be parallel with the foot rail. The head and middle balls should be lined up with the table's center spots, the foot and head spots. Refer to Chapter 8 for the correct placement of the balls in 8-ball, 9-ball and straight pool.

Offensive break shot   *While your aim and objective will vary depending on the pool game, the following basic tips can put some snap in your break stroke, which - unlike the defensive break - is unlike any other stroke in your pool game.*

Stand up a little more. Shift your weight to your front leg. Move your grip back a few inches towards the butt of your cue. Take your cue back slowly, then propel the cue forward quickly, accelerating through the cue ball just as the tip makes contact. The timing of the break shot is critical. Don't forget to take a few feather strokes before propelling the cue forward; it helps hone accuracy and builds momentum.

Some players lurch their bodies forward to enhance this acceleration. In some cases this sympathetic motion results in added thrust and power. But if this movement isn't choreographed correctly, the result is calamitous: a miscue or a complete miss; a cue ball that flies up and smashes a light; a scratch or an errant cue ball. These breaks can appear impressive, but more often than not they compromise precision.

If you're a beginner, use either the head or a side rail for support. Place the cue ball a few inches from the rail to the right or left of the long string (middle). Form a rail bridge. Using a plain ball hit, drive the cue ball into the one ball as full as you can. This break shot might not carve up the pack like a thanksgiving turkey, but until your stroke improves, your main focus is to keep the cue ball on the playing surface while hitting the rack firmly enough to get a few balls to the rails. And don't be surprised if you make a ball or two in the process. Remember to chalk up.

The better your offensive break becomes, the more you'll want to invest in a good **break cue**. Breaking with your playing cue isn't advisable as the shock of the impact can flatten your perfectly domed tip, pop it off or worse, damage the cue's joint.

When selecting a break stick, some players prefer a heavier one to give them more brawn on the break. Many look for a lighter cue to give them added speed and sensitivity. Select the stick that best suits your style and game of preference.

Key to every offensive break

After every offensive break, eyeball the way the balls are reacting. If you're not getting the right action, and you're convinced it's not your technical execution, try something new. Move the cue ball closer to the rail. Try breaking with the cue ball closer to the long string. If you're breaking on an angle with your cue ball to the left of center, change the contact point: aim the cue ball to contact the front ball a hair to the left of center – which makes the cue ball snap right. (This often gets the balls moving.) Experiment hitting a ball in the second or third row: some top 8-ballers have observed that head ball breaks are less effective if the balls, weather (humidity) and playing conditions are less than ideal. Always keep in mind that you want a break shot that gets maximum action with minimum risk. Accuracy pockets more balls than power: aim for consistent results.

ins the lag or lot (usually a coin
opening break or assigning it to

ent pick a side of the table and a
er side of the table on the head
r less at the same time) shoot
ble at a medium-soft speed so it
s back to (hopefully) freeze on
ose ball is closest to the head
es it or if both balls rebound
est to the head rail wins. If the

ose the lag if

your opponent's side of the

cushion or touches the long

- your ball drops into a pocket or jumps off the table

RAIL, BREAKOUT AND BASIC BANK SHOTS

Rail shot   If the object ball is frozen to the cushion about a foot or so away, aim to hit the object ball and the cushion simultaneously. And don't forget to follow through. If the angle is steep and requires a very thin cut, use a little bit of inside siding.

If you must pocket this shot down the cushion and past a side pocket, then aim to hit the rail a hair before contacting the object ball to help the object ball avoid hitting the horn or jaw of the side pocket. Keep in mind that any time the cue ball strikes a rail first some energy or spin is absorbed from the cue ball. This will affect the position of your cue ball after contact. Adjust your speed accordingly.

If the cue ball and the object ball and the pocket are in a straight line, try a medium-soft hit with a half-tip of inside siding. The spin makes the object ball hug the cushion all the way down until it drops into the pocket. If this shot is slightly off the rail, try a marginally firmer hit to keep the object ball on line.

Rail-first   If your object ball is sitting over the hole and you haven't got the angle to send the cue ball to the other end of the table for your next shot, hit it rail-first: pocket the object ball with the rebounding cue ball. Aim so that the cue ball bounces off the cushion and glances off the edge of the object ball. A thinner cut will make the cue ball travel farther after contact. On a straight-in shot, a bit of outside English will send *whitey* to the cushion and sprinting down table for your next shot.

Clusters and the breakout shot   A cluster is a grouping of balls. They're useful when you want to play safe; concealing the cue ball behind a gang of balls is a devilish defense. But when one of your key balls is imprisoned in a cluster, this can be very troublesome, indeed. In this case, you will need to play a **breakout shot**. This is a shot where, after pocketing an object ball, the cue ball bounces your ball or balls out of a cluster, off a rail or any other spot that's ruinous to your runout.

When lining up a breakout shot:

- use the natural or altered path of the cue ball after contact to break out or move balls
- ensure that you have enough speed and just enough fullness to glance off the object ball most likely to bounce the others apart. If the cue ball rolls into the middle of a cluster of balls without the energy to beat 'em – it might just join 'em. After all, you want a break out – not a break in!

 Eyeball a cluster the way you would a flea market: they often contain hidden treasures. Caroms, billiards or combinations like to play hide-and-seek. Don't see it yet? Look again. What if you were to hit it the shot rail-first?

Basic bank shot   When your object ball is bounced into the pocket off a cushion, it's called a bank shot. Under controlled conditions the angle of incidence or **angle in** (the angle at which the cue ball approaches the cushion) should equal the rebound angle or **angle out** (the angle at which the cue ball departs from the

The bank shot system

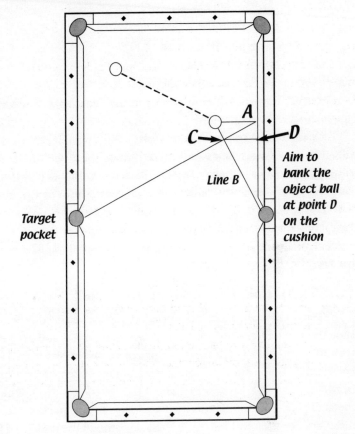

Target pocket

Line B

Aim to bank the object ball at point D on the cushion

cushion). However, variables such as speed and the condition of the cushion, weather and cloth will have a direct effect on the angle out. So, use the fable of angle in and angle out as a reference, not a rule.

Basic bank system

- Draw a straight line from the object ball to the cushion. That gives you **point A**.
- Draw a line from the object ball to the pocket directly opposite to your target pocket. That gives you **line B**.
- Walk around the table to the target pocket and, using your cue, establish a line that runs from the mouth of the target pocket to point A. Call the point where these two lines intersect **point C**.

49

- Draw a line from point C to the cushion. Call that **point D**.
- To make that bank shot, use a plain ball hit at medium speed (as a good reference shot) and *aim the object ball into the cushion at point D*. Use two match sticks to help you visualize points A and D.

Variables affecting the bank shot

Speed   A hard stroke produces a narrower angle of rebound. A soft stroke widens or lengthens this angle.

Center and non-center ball hits   Hit a plain ball at medium speed and the angle in should roughly equal the angle out. Follow (topspin) imparts draw (reverse spin) to the object ball. This narrows or shortens the bank. Draw imparts follow to the object ball. This widens or lengthens the bank. Left English imparts right English to the object ball. Right English imparts Left English to the object ball. Inside siding shortens the bank. Outside siding lengthens the bank.

COMBINATION, CAROM AND BILLIARD SHOTS

Two-ball combination shots   On a two-ball combination shot, the cue ball hits one object ball, which then hits and pockets a second object ball. There are two types of combinations: frozen (the balls in the combination are touching) and non-frozen (there's space between the balls). Factors that affect the outcome of this shot are the set-up of the combination with relation to the pocket and the distances between the balls. A line drawn through the middle of two touching balls is called the **line of centers**.

Here's how to tell whether a combination is "wired" (a sure thing), "on" (possible with an adjustment), or a figment of a tormented imagination.

If a combination is

Frozen, near the pocket and lined up perfectly with center pocket   If the line of centers points into the pocket, then you have a generous target area: the cue ball can strike the first object ball almost anywhere and the second object ball rockets straight into the pocket. Miss this, as they say in the poolroom, and there oughta be an inquiry.

Frozen, lined up with but a few feet from the pocket
Your margin of error decreases. With a center ball contact, you must hit a precise point of impact because of the variable of throw. Even if the line of centers points into the pocket, when a cue ball cuts two frozen balls, the second object ball may be thrown off-line. The softer the hit, the more the ball will be thrown. The greater the distance, the greater the affect of throw. Depending on the distance, sometimes a firm hit is enough to tackle this variable. If not, you'll need to apply a little English to tame the throw.

Frozen but not exactly lined up with the pocket It's still possible to make the shot if you adjust your aim. Determine where the line of centers is pointing. Is it to the left or the right of the pocket? If it's pointing to the right, without an adjustment, the second object ball will veer to the right of the pocket – and into the cushion. To make this shot (with a center ball hit), aim the cue ball to contact the first ball to the right of center. When you cut this first ball to the left, it will pull the second ball to the left - and into the pocket. Presto! *Adjust your aim in the direction of the line of centers.* The more you cut the shot to the right, the more it throws to the left. Also, if a lot of throw is needed, there must be enough distance between the second object ball and the pocket for the throw to take effect. Note: You can still throw in a combo if the balls are slightly apart.

Non-frozen Ideally, you want the cue ball and the balls in the combination to be fairly close together and lined up at easy angles. Cutting (thinner contact) or driving (fuller contact) the first object ball into a second object ball sitting over the pocket also gives you a reasonable margin of error. If, however, the second ball is a few feet from the pocket or the first ball is a good distance from the second or the cue ball is a distance from the combo, then you're going to have to judge the shot. Lift your cue over the combination and visualize exactly what must happen to pocket the shot. If pocketing the second object ball is fiction rather than fact, play safe!

To execute a non-frozen combination

1.   Temporarily, take the cue ball out of the equation.

2. Visualize a ghost ball behind the second object ball. The ghost ball acts as your imaginary first object ball. This is where the first object ball must be on impact to pocket the second object ball.

3. Now, go to the first object ball and pretend it's the cue ball. Take a few (careful) feather strokes as if you were preparing to sink the second object ball with it.

4. Go back to the real cue ball. Using the same method, establish where you must aim the cue ball to send the first object ball to the correct point on the second object ball.

5. When executing a non-frozen combination, take the pocket out of the equation and approach it as if it were a single-ball shot. Focus exclusively on the cue ball and first object ball and pretend the second object ball is the pocket. As in any single-ball shot – when you're pulling the trigger, lock your eyes on the first object ball and resist the urge to watch what the second ball is doing upon contact. Aiming through the cue ball to a point beyond the rail will help you stay down on the shot.

Caroms (also called kiss shots) A carom is a shot where the cue ball hits an object ball into a second or "helper" ball, as it's called, in such a way that the object ball kisses *in* the pocket *off* the helper ball.

To line up a carom shot

- First establish a target line that runs from the pocket and grazes the edge of the helper ball (the edge that your object ball will hit).
- Freeze a ghost ball to the helper ball so that their line of centers forms a 90° angle with the target line.
- Now, judge where the cue ball must contact the object ball to send it into that ghost ball position.
- Striking the cue ball in the center at medium speed, aim the cue ball so that the object ball hits the helper ball at this point. The object ball will then glance off the helper ball, travel along the right angle target line and drop into the pocket. Aiming through the cue ball at a point beyond the rail will aid the execution of the shot.

The kiss shot

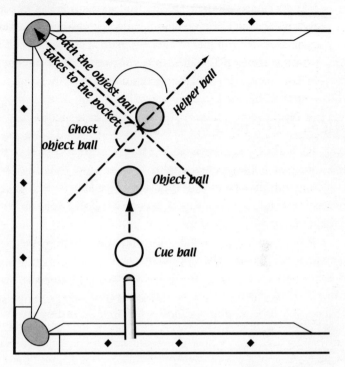

Path the object ball takes to the pocket

Helper ball

Ghost object ball

Object ball

Cue ball

- Use what you know about ball reactions with center and non-center ball hits. With a little experience, you'll also be able to adjust the angles and speed to play crowd-pleasing caroms every time.

Billiards   Technically a carom, a billiard is a shot where the cue ball glances off (and sometimes) pockets a helper ball, then sinks your object ball.

When lining up a billiard shot:

- Remember, if you strike a cue ball in the center at medium speed, the cue ball will glance off the object ball along a right-angle line.
- Determine where you need to contact the object ball to sink it (point of impact).

- Establish the path that the cue ball will take after contact with the helper ball. Does it lead to the point of impact on your object ball? If not, use what you know about center and non-center ball hits to alter the path that the cue ball takes after contact. Try adjusting your speed and thickness of contact and you'll be making billiards that you never thought possible.

KICK, JUMP, MASSÉ AND SWERVE SHOTS

Kick shot   Kicking a ball is a term that refers to a shot where the cue ball makes contact with the cushion (rail-first) before colliding with the object ball. Typically a kick shot is used to get out of a safety or hook, or as a way of making a ball that you can only see a thin fraction of.

When you have a partially obstructed ball, here's a handy kick trick that will amaze your opponents. Using your cue, establish the point of impact on your object ball and extend that imaginary line to the rail. How many inches would you say that line is? Six? Now extend that line another six inches out to a point beyond the rail. Aim at that ghost point and, with the right hit (try medium paced), your cue ball should contact the spot that kicks in your object ball.

When learning the trick shot

- Aim the cue ball at one of the two long rails and try and scratch in a corner pocket and then a side pocket. When you can pocket the cue ball a few times, position another ball over the corner pocket and then side pocket and repeat this exercise, shooting the one-rail corner and side kicks.
- Try experimenting with a few non-center hits on the cue ball at the same speed. Notice how the path of the cue ball changes coming off the cushion. With practice, you'll learn to adjust where the cue ball contacts the cushion to kick that ball in. Now try a few shots moving the object ball farther from the pocket. Try different speeds. Notice how a soft hit widens the angle of rebound and a firm hit narrows it.

Jump shot   When you're hooked or partially hooked and can't get to the spot on the cushion to hit your object ball, under certain conditions, you could jump the cue ball over the edge of an obstructing ball. For the record, shovelling under the cue ball to lift it up into the air is called a scoop shot – and it's a foul. A legal jump shot is stroked down into the slate, which causes the cue ball to bounce up and over the obstructing ball. The cue ball then hits, and hopefully pockets, your object ball.

To jump a ball

- Position your body sideways and elevate the butt of your cue. Your left foot (if you're right-handed) is forward. The instep of your right foot and stroking arm are along the line of aim. Use the same elevated bridge you would use to stroke over a ball.
- The cueing action is unique from a typical shot. When jumping the cue ball, relax your grip and toss or throw the cue through the bottom of the cue ball, clipping the follow-through. Aim to strike down through the cue ball at about one and a half to two full tips below center. Experiment with the elevation to get the action just right.
- Although full ball clearances are possible, they're extremely difficult. In the beginning, only attempt to clear the edge of a ball. When the cue ball is a few inches from the cushion, it's easier to jump: you can position your bridge on the rail and the added height aids your stroke and stance. Also, don't jump the cue ball unless the minimum distance between the cue ball and the obstructing ball is 30 cm (12 in.). The farther the distance between the object ball and the cue ball, the more force and control you'll need to keep the appropriate trajectory on the cue ball.
- To jump a ball it helps to have a jump cue. This is a cue that's been shortened and engineered to jump a cue ball. If you don't have one, try choking up on your playing cue: move your grip hand a good 15 cm (6 in.) toward the joint. Personalize this distance.

Massé shot   To make the cue ball curve around obstructing balls, elevate your bridge hand and the butt of your cue and get ready to apply some English. But before you begin, a word of warning: players at all skill levels practicing massés tend to make room owners very nervous. Like the jump shot, improper execution often results in a torn or dinged cloth. So please, proceed with caution.

If you want to curve the cue ball to the left, use left English. Use right English if you want to curve to the right. Imagine the cue ball as the face of a clock. Aiming at 3:00 will give you extreme right English; 9:00 extreme left English. If you hit the cue ball below centre this delays the curve. For a more pronounced effect, lift the butt end of your cue higher still. If you want to hasten the curve, hit above center. The massé shot demands a great deal of feel and a well-timed release. Don't overpower the shot. Control the release; don't jab or poke, but stroke down through the cue ball.

Keep those fingers of your bridge hand solid on the cloth.

Swerve   If a quarter or half of an obstructing ball is blocking your object ball, ransack your arsenal for the mini-massé. You don't want a full curve, just a little swerve to get past the edge of the ball.

Keeping your bridge hand slightly elevated and planted, raise the butt of your cue and stroke downward on the side of the cue ball. It's a slow and controlled release that will make the English take and the cue ball swerve around the obstructing ball to hit – and with practice – pocket your object ball.

When massés become second nature, the **grand massé shot** beckons. Elevate your cue until it's straight, practically perpendicular with the table. Aim at 6:00 and release the cue through the bottom of the cue ball. Watch it curve and reverse back toward you. Set up the cue ball and an object ball beside each other but not touching over the mouth of the pocket. Massé the cue ball so that it curves back to pocket the neighboring object ball. It's an extraordinary shot!

Chapter Six

Basic strategy

PATTERNS

A pattern is a plan of attack; it's a choreographed runout. After the balls have been broken, a player examines the layout of the balls, determines a correct order to shoot the balls in (depending on the game, of course) and decides how to run out.

On occasion the balls are laid out so that the runout is a no-brainer. Natural rolls or a series of easy stop or stun shots lead the cue ball to your next ball. This is also called "a broom-stick runout" (it's so easy you could run out with a broomstick). Usually, the layout is a little more complicated and involves figuring out how to break up clusters or get balls off the rails as soon as possible in the game.

Select your order of shots carefully; the late stages of a runout are the most critical. The last thing you want to do is make most of the balls and mess up, leaving your opponent with the game ball to shoot (9-ball) or with a lot less traffic (8-ball) to hinder his runout.

Patterns will change every time balls are moved about, or you miss position on one of your balls. You may have to restructure a few times within the course of a game. If the new table layout is fraught with complications, make what you can and play defensively. Better safe than sorry. Here's something to look forward to: the more you play, the more you'll begin to see repeating patterns. Invest in a good broomstick!

A runout is pocketing a ball or balls on the break, then running the rest of your balls in the same turn.

POSITIONAL PLAY

Pocketing balls, for a pool player, is like eating salted peanuts – one is never enough. The novelty of making a few shots now and then gives way to a strong desire to run the table. And this can only happen by learning to control the cue ball.

Positional play begins with three principles:

1. Pocket the object ball.
2. Plan what ball to shoot next.
3. Leave the cue ball so that you have a clear, well-positioned shot on your next ball.

On any shot involving an angle, wherever possible, position the cue ball using the **natural roll**. To do this you must ensure that the cue ball is situated on the right side of the object ball: on the angle that will send the cue ball towards your next object ball after sinking the first one. This is basic pool strategy.

With cue ball in hand, before placing it anywhere, look at your next ball. If your object ball is six inches straight out from the side pocket, and your next ball is near the foot rail, don't mindlessly line up the cue ball for an easy straight-in shot in the side. On a plain ball hit, the cue ball will either travel forward or stop somewhere around the original position of the object ball. Often this is far from your ideal position. First lesson in controlling the cue ball: *think before you shoot*. Second lesson: *keep it simple*.

On this shot, the proper spot for the cue ball is on an angle that sits below the object ball. The natural roll after contact takes it up table for your next shot.

Pinpoint versus area position   In full-rack games (15 balls) such as 8-ball, you'll often run into high traffic – a lot of blocking balls that reduce the playing surface and limit your positional options. In

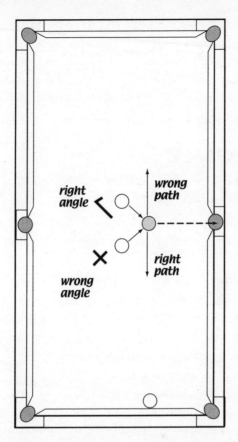

Keep it simple: Get the cue ball on the right side of the object ball for natural position on your next shot.

these instances, in order to get a clear shot (where you can see both edges) on your next ball, you must play the cue ball to a **specific point** on the table, sometimes by altering its natural path with a non-center ball hit. This is called playing **pinpoint position**. The risk on this shot is high because if you lose *whitey* by a margin as small as an eighth of a ball, you could be hooked solidly on your next shot. Study these kinds of limited-path shots carefully. In many instances it just isn't physically possible to get the cue ball to that spot, so play safe!

If the balls are spread out, you can play the cue ball into a larger area to get shape on your next ball. This is called playing **area position**.

Visualize the area between the inside edges of the cue ball, your object ball, your next ball and the relevant surrounding balls. Shade this area mentally, if you must. How will you get the cue ball into this area? Will a natural roll take you there or must you alter the path of the cue ball? If an angle is involved, do you also have to worry about getting on the right side of your next ball to prolong your run?

Defensive strategy is as much a part of pool as football, hockey or any other sport – if you want to win, that is!

SAFETY PLAY

When you bury the cue ball so that your opponent doesn't have a clear shot on her object ball, this is called a **hook** or a **snooker**. Safety play involves strategically positioning the cue ball so that your opponent is reacting instead of attacking. In this way you maintain control of the game.

In your travels you may encounter a few trigger-happy opponents who'll question your scruples if you don't shoot at everything, regardless of whether you have something to shoot at or not. Execute a skilful hook and they'll cry, "Unfair! Dirty pool." In this case, smile and let your opponent rant. She will send *whitey* on a fool's errand: bust up the pack gladly; free up your trouble balls; foul or miss giving you the game, or a huge edge at least. The simple rule: If you don't have a shot … *better safe than stupid!*

To execute a safety

1. Survey the table. Look for a clever hiding spot for the cue ball, somewhere your opponent can't pocket a ball or hit the ball and leave you hooked on your next shot. (This is called a **return safety**.) Now, put yourself in your opponent's shoes and ask how you would get out of this hook. If blocking balls make his escape worthy of Houdini's talent, you've picked your spot well.

2.   Locate the perfect object ball. Controlling the cue ball with speed or a center or non-center ball hit, glance off the edge of this object ball and bury the cue ball behind a ball or better yet, a cluster of balls. Before you shoot, don't forget to assess how much of the cue ball should make contact with the object ball, since this will affect the distance that the cue ball travels after contact.

Two-way shot   The two-way is a shot made with an offensive or defensive strategy in mind. For example:An 8-baller can minimize the risk of a low-percentage shot by playing it two ways. If you are successful in pocketing it, the cue ball is favorably positioned for their next ball; in the event of a miss, the leave is safe for the incoming player.

In 9-ball, you'll win automatically if you can pocket your lowest numbered ball with a hit that sends the cue ball to legally pocket the 9-ball after contact.

In straight pool, you'll play two-way shots that involve pocketing your called ball and causing the cue ball to bump the 15th ball into the perfect "break-ball" position.

Look for two-way shots as they allow you to

- eliminate trouble spots (8-ball, straight pool).
- minimize the risk of shooting a low-percentage shot (8-ball, straight pool).
- win instantly (9-ball). Still, weigh out the risk involved. If your chances of running out are greater than executing a tricky carom, stay with your original plan.

Chapter Seven

Playing 8-ball, 9-ball and 14.1 straight pool

While there's an exhaustive selection of pool games, 8-ball, 9-ball and straight pool (14.1) are core disciplines that share a special relationship. Beginners usually start with 8-ball; it's a popular **full-rack** game (15 balls) that's great for nurturing the basics. Fast and flirty, 9-ball is a **partial-rack** game (9 balls) that develops a command of positional play. Straight pool, a **multi-rack** game, teaches breaking skills, safety strategy, and patience and finesse. Finally, players return to 8-ball with a fortified arsenal of shots and strategies, and the subtlety to play any pool game well.

RULES AND STRATEGIES FOR 8-BALL

In the early 1900s, the Brunswick-Balke-Collender Company, the venerable manufacturer of bowling and billiard equipment, invented a new pool game called BBC Co. pool. Fun and easy to learn, this variation was developed to promote BBC's quality tables and a new line of balls.

The objective of BBC Co. pool was to pocket one group of balls – either seven red or seven yellow – before sinking a solid black to win. The game took off. The balls did not. Rather than purchase the new novelty balls, players just racked up the traditional stripes and solids and sunk the 8-ball to win. By the 1920s, players were already calling the game by the name 8-ball.

Today the game, also known as Stripes and Solids, Highs and Lows, Bigs and Littles and Boston, has grown into the most popular casual and amateur tournament and league competition pool game.

The objective To pocket all of the numbered balls in your group – either the solid balls (1 to 7) or the striped balls (9 to 15) – before legally pocketing the black 8-ball to win.

The rack Gather all 15 balls in a triangle with the head ball on the foot spot. Placing the 1-ball in front is a courtesy, but positioning a stripe in this position can be visually more offsetting for your opponent. The 8-ball must be racked in the middle. The corner balls (most likely to drop on the break) must alternate. Ensure there's a stripe in one back corner and a solid in the other.

Call shots Except for the break, 8-ball is a "called shot" game. If a shot is obvious, you don't have to say anything. If the shot is unclear, however, you must call the object ball and the intended pocket. (You're not obliged to give your opponent the details of how it will get there.) In certain leagues you must always call the 8-ball by marking the pocket with a coaster. Forget to do this and you'll lose. Call all bank shots, combination, billiard and carom shots, as they are not considered obvious.

The break is not considered a called shot. Any legally pocketed numbered balls are scored in favor of the breaker.

In order for the break to be a legal shot

- the cue ball must make contact with a numbered ball in the rack and
- at least one ball must be pocketed after contact, and/or
- at least four numbered balls must be driven to a rail. Failure to do so results in a foul.

The incoming player is now awarded a few choices: play the table as lies, or have the balls reracked, and break or let the offending player break again.

If a player **scratches** on the break, the incoming player receives cue ball in hand but must place the cue ball behind the head string and shoot up table (towards the foot rail). Any pocketed balls stay down.

If the **8-ball is pocketed on the break**, officially (and in some league formats) you don't win. The breaker can either ask for a rerack or have the 8-ball spotted (foot spot) and continue shooting. If there's a ball on the foot spot, refer to "spotting balls" in Appendix 2.

In a format where you can't win by pocketing the 8-ball on the snap, you also can't lose by making the black and scratching. If this happens, the incoming player has the choice of a rerack or having the 8-ball spotted and playing on, placing the cue ball behind the head string and shooting up table (towards the foot rail).

If you're not playing for a trophy, it's much more fun to count a pocketed 8-ball as an instant win. Some bar players insist that if any numbered balls go down with the 8-ball, this is an automatic loss. This doesn't make sense. The break isn't a call shot: you fluked the 8-ball, so any other numbered balls should count as well. Play by these rules, however, and sinking the 8-ball and the cue ball on the same break stroke is also an instant loss.

How to break in 8-ball   The 8-ball break is an open rather than safety break. Your goals are to:

1.   create as much action as possible (this means getting the balls moving, so at least one ball is pocketed and the rest are spread out advantageously), and
2.   leave the cue ball in the center of the table. You have the most options from this position.

Pocketing at least one ball offers two key advantages: the choice of group, which leaves your opponent with more trouble spots, and a shot at running out.

The secret to a great 8-ball break is to drive the cue ball into the pack with as much speed and force, as you're able to control. Focus on accuracy: your speed will build with time and confidence. Begin by placing the cue ball 15 to 20 cm (6 to 8 in.) from the side rail (behind the head string, to the left or right of the long string). Form a loop bridge. This is a power stroke that requires maximum support and guidance; you won't get that from an open bridge. Using a center ball, or a half-tip below center break, aim to contact the apex ball as squarely as the round balls will allow. Beginners may prefer to use a rail bridge and break from the side or head rail for added support.

As with any opening break, it's important to remember that every set of balls and every table is different. So, if this particular break isn't getting the desired action, try changing the cue ball to apex ball contact or keep moving the cue ball until you find the magic spot.

Open table   Regardless of what balls have been pocketed on the break shot, it's still **open table**; you can shoot a stripe or a solid ball. If you legally pocket a called stripe or solid, you're committed to that group for the duration of that game.

Choosing a group   Once the balls have been scattered, nine out of 10 times there's a duck sitting right over a hole. While beginners are all out to shoot this ball first, experienced players look for another shot, even if it's slightly more difficult. They'll want to leave the hangers; it's what they'll call an **insurance ball**, an easy shot that they can always come back to later. (Remember, a ball over the pocket offers multiple points of impact. By altering your aim, speed or hit, you can get the cue ball to a variety of spots on the table. This can save your bacon if you run into trouble.)

To choose the right group in 8-ball you must learn to read the balls forward from the break and backward from the black. Study the table and ask yourself the following questions:

- Where are the trouble spots? Balls in clusters, balls along the rails, balls in dead combinations? Can I reasonably get to the trouble spots and how soon?
- How does the table play? Is the cloth playing fast or slow? Are the rails lively or dead? Does the table drift to one side? Will this affect my banks or breakouts?
- What balls are blocking the pockets?
- Where is the black ball? Is it hanging precariously over a pocket? What pockets will the 8-ball go into? Where's my key ball – the ball that takes me to the right position on the 8-ball?
- Can I run out? Should I even try running out?
- If not, which ball gives me the most impenetrable safety shot?

Legal versus foul shots   The break and open table shots have their own peculiarities. On all other shots, in order to be legal, the shooter must:

1.   hit one of his own balls first, either stripes or solids, *and*
2.   pocket the called numbered ball in the intended pocket, *or*
3.   cause a ball (either the cue ball or any numbered ball) to hit a cushion after contact.

Note: if you sink your called solid in the called pocket and any stripes or unintended solids are made in the process, this is not a foul or loss of turn; keep shooting.

Non-tournament players may find point 3 confusing; it's nearly never observed in casual play. This might be easier to grasp through a few typical examples:

- Your object ball rolls towards the pocket, but doesn't drop. Nor does it touch a cushion or pocket horn. To make matters worse, your cue ball fails to reach a cushion or bounce another ball into a cushion after contact. This is a full-fledged foul.
- You're hooked behind one of your opponent's balls. You shoot the cue ball softly into the cushion; it rolls off the cushion and hits your buried object ball, but fails to drive your object ball or the cue ball to the cushion after contact. This is a foul.
- Many social 8-ballers play safe by rolling the cue ball softly to freeze it behind one of their balls without causing a ball to hit a rail after contact. While this is a legal safety in snooker, in any pocket billiards game, this is a foul.

Foul penalties   Again, this wonderful rule may seem odd to those who have been weaned on bar pool. When a foul has been committed, the offending player loses his turn *and* the incoming player is awarded **cue ball in hand**. This means the incoming player can take the cue ball and place it anywhere on the table and shoot in any direction (providing the foul hasn't been committed on the break).

Typical loss of turn
- failing to pocket your legal object ball on a legal stroke
- making your legal object ball in the wrong pocket
- sinking the wrong ball (in your own group)

Typical fouls
- hitting the black first when you still have numbered balls on the table
- knocking any numbered balls off the table (jumped balls aren't spotted)

66

- hitting a ball from your opponent's group first
- scratching the cue ball on the break

Game over The black ball must be pocketed on a clean stroke. While you still have numbered balls on the table, consider it a poison ball. Note that if you legally pocket your last ball and hook yourself on the black, this isn't a loss if you fail to hit it. It's a foul; the incoming player receives ball in hand. Nevertheless, it is all over but the crying if you

- jump the 8-ball off the table
- pocket the 8-ball and the cue ball in the same stroke (except on the break)
- pocket the 8-ball in a pocket you didn't nominate
- pocket the 8-ball when it isn't your legal object ball
- fail to satisfy the requirements for a legal shot when shooting the 8-ball (if you miss, a ball had better hit a cushion after contact)

Legal combinations The shooter is allowed to play a two-ball combination if the balls are from the same group, stripes or solids. In a legal three-ball combination, the first object ball that the cue ball contacts and the called object ball must be from the same group. It doesn't matter what's sandwiched in the middle.

If the table is open, you can legally shoot a ball from one group into a called ball from the opposing group, in an effort to pocket the called stripe or solid. If you pocket the called ball, you continue shooting that group. If you miss, you lose your turn and the table is still open for the incoming player. If you miss the called ball and pocket the first object ball in the combination, you lose your turn. Any pocketed balls stay down and the table is still open.

Safety shots While players like to think they can run out every game, it's impossible. Every break shot will yield a unique layout. How you approach this table will depend on one thing: are you having fun or playing to win?

If you can't run out, know that the worst thing you can do in 8-ball (particularly against a skilled player) is to make five or six of your balls and miss, leaving one numbered ball and the black. When this happens, the odds of winning belong to your opponent.

With your balls out of the way, there is less traffic. You've removed blocking balls and freed up key pockets and playing surface, which makes playing position a lot easier for your opponent. Furthermore, even if your opponent can't run out, she will have a glut of ways to hook you solidly. So, if you don't have a shot, play safe: you'll maintain control in the game and keep your opponent reacting until she makes the fatal error that puts you back in the balls.

If your opponent fouls and you receive cue ball in hand, unless it's necessary, don't waste this by shooting an obvious ball. Take a trouble ball – one that's on the rail or a shot that might otherwise require you to play pinpoint position. Study the table. See if you can place the cue ball so that the angle will send it to break up or move key balls.

The *safety* shot In 8-ball, you can declare "safety": sink an object ball in your own group to leave the cue ball safe after contact, then relinquish your turn at the table. This tactical gem can turn you into the puppeteer and your opponent, the puppet. If, however, you forget to call "safety," any pocketed balls stay down and you're obliged to shoot again.

RULES AND STRATEGIES FOR 9-BALL

Lights! Camera! Action! Television loves 9-ball. With the exception of snooker, 9-ball is the most avidly broadcast cue sport discipline. It's sexy, exciting, fast-paced: the signature elements of a pop music video.

This game is based on rotation. It's a full-rack pool game where the balls are pocketed in numerical sequence. Positional play is key, but luck definitely sweetens the pot. It's not a "called shot" game, per se. Fluke the 9-ball in on the snap or slop it in accidentally and you win: instant gratification!

The objective To hit the lowest numbered ball on the table. While the cue ball must contact the balls (1 through 9) in order, you aren't limited to pocketing them in numerical sequence. Another unique point: the 9-ball is your money ball. Pocket it legally, intentionally or unintentionally, at any point in the game in a combination, carom, billiard or as a legal object ball and you win.

The rack The game is a partial-rack game. Use the balls numbered 1 through 8 (solids) and the striped 9. To freeze the balls together, don't use the plastic diamonds. You don't have enough room to get your fingers behind the balls to push them forward. If no high-tech pro rack is available, reach for the standard triangle rack. The 1-ball must be racked in front and sit on the foot spot; the 9-ball must be racked in the middle.

Ensure that all of the balls are touching, particularly the first three. Never break if the head ball isn't frozen to both balls behind it. Always check to make sure the 1-ball is on the foot spot and that the rack is correctly aligned. You should be able to draw a straight line through the middles of the 1-ball, 9-ball, back point ball and both spots or diamonds that mark the center of the table.

The break In order for a break shot to be legal the breaker must

1. hit the 1-ball first, and
2. pocket at least one ball on the break, or
3. drive at least four numbered balls to the rail.

If the breaker scratches on the break or sends the cue ball flying off the table, it's a foul. The incoming player takes cue ball in hand and places it anywhere on the table and can shoot in any direction. If a numbered ball is jumped, it's a foul. Any jumped balls are not spotted (place them into a pocket) unless it's the 9-ball. The 9-ball is spotted on the foot spot. If there's a ball on the foot spot, refer to "Spotting balls" in Appendix 2.

How to break in 9-ball With only nine balls on the table, the break is a critical shot. If a few balls drop on the break, watch how quickly a skilled shotmaker can run table or ride the 9 (play a combination by shooting a solid ball into the 9-ball to pocket it).

Your goals on the 9-ball break are to

1. make at least one ball
2. leave the cue ball in the center of the table, and
3. leave the cue ball and the 1-ball in the same area.

If you make the 9-ball on the break you automatically win. By aiming to contact the head ball off-center (same side as your angle of approach), you can snap the 9-ball in the foot-rail corner pocket. Experiment with this break if you must, but do so at your own risk. This is a low-percentage shot: If any other ball but the 9-ball drops, this break sends the cue ball and 1-ball to opposite ends of the table, leaving you with a poor position on the 1-ball.

Top 9-ballers have found that breaking from the side rails yields the highest odds of making balls on the break and possibly sinking the 9-ball. This position for the break was so effective that the men's pro tour banned it. Players were restricted to breaking from the box (the area behind the head string between the first and third diamonds on the head rail).

For a winning break, place the cue ball (three to five centimetres) from the side rail. With nothing fancier than a center-ball hit, propel the cue ball into the 1-ball as full in the face as you can. Use the rail (and a firm rail bridge) for added support. Some players address the cue ball below center in their feather strokes, but upon contact, the tip of their cue comes up slightly to strike and accelerate through the middle of the cue ball. Unless there's interference from other balls, this break tends to send the corner balls toward (and hopefully in) the corner pockets and the 1-ball towards the side pocket. The cue ball heels obediently in the middle of the table, awaiting your next command.

If this break isn't working, you're going to have to do what all of the pros do: start fiddling. Again, playing conditions vary from table to table – indeed, from morning session to evening session. Start moving the cue ball to find a position behind the head string that will cut that diamond. There's a spot on every table where the balls will break best. Sometimes you'll be playing with dead balls on a dead table. If this is the case, you may not have the luxury of playing shape on the 1-ball; you're all out to make one ball on the break. There are no easy formulas. Just keep searching for the magic spot.

Push shot   Following a legal break, the shooter can pushout. This means, the shooter has the option of pushing (rolling) the cue ball to a more advantageous location on the table. On this shot, the shooter isn't required to hit another ball or a rail after contacting a numbered ball either. The incoming player then has the option of shooting, or declining a turn by asking you to shoot again.

Before playing this shot, you must declare "push." If you forget to do so, it will be considered a normal shot.

Generally pushouts are played after the break shot when a player has hooked himself or has a lousy shot on the lowest numbered ball. Depending on the layout of the balls, a well-played push shot can offer all kinds of tactical benefits. Some players push the cue ball out to a location where their opponents are almost certain to give up the shot. For instance, a skilled banker might push the cue ball out near a rail. When his opponent says, "Shoot again," he confidently banks the 1-ball and continues shooting.

When pushing out, look to see whether you can set up a hidden gem of a shot (a carom or a billiard) that your opponent might not see. You may also want to play a push shot that intentionally locks up a key ball; this complicates the runout pattern for the incoming player.

Any balls pocketed on push shots stay down – unless it's the 9-ball, which is spotted on the foot spot.

Foul versus legal shots   For a shot to be legal, the shooter must

1.   hit the lowest numbered ball first, and
2.   pocket at least one ball, or
3.   hit a rail (either a numbered ball or the cue ball) after the cue ball makes contact with the object ball.

Any illegally pocketed or jumped balls remain down except for the 9-ball, which is spotted on the foot spot. If you knock the 9-ball off the table, unlike 8-ball, this doesn't end the game – just your turn. The 9-ball is spotted and the incoming player receives ball in hand. If you send the 9-ball into orbit but it lands back on the playing surface without incident, strike up the band and play on. Also, if you make the 9-ball and another numbered ball drops with it – you still win.

If you don't have a shot on the lowest numbered ball, take a look at where the 9-ball is. If it's sitting over a pocket you may want to pocket the 9-ball. This is technically a foul and your opponent is awarded ball in hand, but you can relax in your chair knowing the 9-ball is much safer on the foot spot.

Typical 9-ball fouls

- A ball doesn't hit a rail after contact. Let's say you're on the 3-ball but it's hooked behind the 7-ball. Remember when shooting rail first that it isn't enough to hit the 3-ball. After contact, a ball (the cue ball, the 3-ball or any other numbered ball) must be driven to a cushion.
- Bad hits: the first ball that the cue ball contacts isn't the lowest numbered ball on the table
- Playing an undeclared push shot unless you've pushed the cue ball into the 1-ball – the lowest numbered ball – and hit a rail after contact.
- Not contacting the 1-ball on the break.

After a foul has been committed, the incoming player receives ball in hand and continues playing by placing the cue ball anywhere on the table and shooting in any direction.

Winning 9-ball In 9-ball you can win by

1. sinking the 9-ball on a legal break, or
2. running the balls in order and pocketing the game-winning 9-ball, or
3. riding the 9: pocketing the 9-ball (intentionally or unintentionally) in a two or even four-ball combination (just hit the lowest numbered ball first), or
4. by hooking your opponent, causing him to commit three consecutive fouls.

Three fouls   In 9-ball, if a player commits three consecutive fouls, it's an automatic loss of game. It's demoralizing and dispiriting (but a deeply gratifying way of winning).

If your opponent has scratched on a shot (possibly following the break) and you don't like the layout, take ball in hand and look for a good safety. If your opponent doesn't legally contact the obstructed object ball, that's foul number two. At this point you must declare, "You're on two." Now, take ball in hand and try to hook him again. If your opponent fails to contact the ball, or doesn't hit a rail after contact, or scratches in the process – this is a third consecutive foul. You win the game instantly.

In order to legally three-foul an opponent, the shooter must give a warning after the second foul and before playing the third hook. (This reminder also seems to work its way under an opponent's skin.) As well, these three fouls must be incurred within the same game and consecutively. If your opponent misses the first two hooks but legally contacts the obstructed object ball on the third try, then the slate is wiped clean.

RULES AND STRATEGIES FOR 14.1

Until the early '70s, 14.1, also called straight pool, was the contest of pool skill that decided the world champion. That is until 9-ball entered the competitive scene in the '60s and quickly changed the face and pace of tournament pocket billiards.

Today, top players still hold the discipline of 14.1 in high regard and consider it to be "pure pool." It's a remarkable game that will hone your shot-making skills, stamina and safety play. Here are a few basic rules and tips, just enough to get you up and running, rack after rack. In fact, you'll soon discover that one of the most addictive qualities of 14.1 is the desire to beat your own high runs.

The objective　The names straight pool and 14.1 *continuous* come from the objective of the game: to run as many balls and straight racks as you can. When 14 balls have been pocketed and only the 15th ball and the cue ball remain, leave them where they lie. Then carefully gather the other 14 balls and load them into the triangle. Rack them without the front (15th) ball and position the rack as if that (ghost) apex ball were sitting on the vacant foot spot.

The 15th ball is called the **break ball**. This is a key ball in straight pool. It's both the last shot of the last rack and your first shot in the new rack. Top 14.1 players take great care to position this ball correctly. They look to leave it where they can play a two-way shot: legally pocket the called 15th ball and, after contact, cause the cue ball to break out their next object ball(s) from the virgin rack. In this manner they can keep shooting. You're not, however, required to pocket your break ball (15th ball). If you don't like the shot, play the cue ball safe; defensive strategy is key in 14.1.

In 14.1 the first player to reach the predetermined point total wins (100 or 150 is a typical tournament point total, 75 points is a reasonable race for a casual contest). One point is awarded for every ball you pocket. If you pocket your object ball and another ball or balls are pocketed unintentionally on the same stroke, you rack up an extra or extra points. You don't have to pocket the balls in any kind of numerical sequence or grouping, but 14.1 is a called shot game, even on the break shot. You don't have to call an obvious shot. Combos, banks, caroms, billiards or balls pocketed off the break are not considered obvious.

The rack The game uses the standard triangle rack: all 15 balls. There's no special apex ball, but the head ball must sit on the foot spot. The 1-ball is positioned in the back right corner (to the racker's right). The 5-ball sits in the back left corner. You can rack the other balls randomly.

When reracking the 14 balls, rack them as if the (missing) apex ball were sitting on the foot spot. If you haven't played a lot of 14.1, pure force of habit may lead you to reach for the break ball and cue ball by accident. Make a metal note to resist this temptation. If this happens, simply put the balls back to where you think they were.

The break: breaking violation versus foul shot Unlike 8-ball and 9-ball, most winners of the lag or coin toss in 14.1 will pass the break shot to their opponent. For a legal straight-pool break, you must:

1. call the ball and pocket and legally execute the shot, *or*
2. cause the cue ball to contact a ball and at least one cushion, and
3. cause two numbered balls to contact a cushion after contact.

Failure to do this is a **breaking violation** punishable by a two-point penalty. The incoming player now has a choice of playing the table as it lies or having the balls reracked and asking the offending player to break again. The three consecutive-foul-rule does not apply on the break shot, but should it happen again, the offending player is docked two points for every failed attempt.

If the breaker scratches on the break, this is a foul. The offending player suffers a one-point penalty (scored as a minus one point). The incoming player takes cue ball in hand behind the head string and must shoot up table (toward the foot rail).

How to break in 14.1 This is a stroke that favors finesse over power: unlike 8-ball and 9-ball, you're not trying to turn the cue ball loose and scatter the pack. You'll need an accurate opening break shot that keeps the rack of balls as intact as possible.

Place the cue ball behind the head string 7 to 15 cm (3 to 6 in.) from the side rail. If you're placing the cue ball to the right of center, apply a little high outside English and aim the cue ball to glance off the edge of the right back corner ball. Snooker players should be familiar with this break shot. Depending on the conditions, medium pace and a quarter-ball contact should get the desired results.

This break will drive at least two numbered balls to the rail – and hopefully back into or near the pack. The cue ball will glance off the edge of the back corner ball, hit the short (foot) rail, the side long rail and travel the length of the table before coming to rest near or on the head rail. You are opening a dialogue of defensive play, hoping that your opponent replies with an error that lets you start amassing points.

Spotting In 14.1, unintentionally pocketed balls are respotted. These are the most common scenarios.

- If the 15th or break ball is in the rack area and interferes with the new rack, the object ball is spotted on the head spot.
- If the cue ball interferes with the new rack, take cue ball in hand behind the head string and shoot up table.
- If your break ball and cue ball interfere with the rack, gather all of the balls and rerack.
- If your cue ball is in the rack area and the break ball is behind the head string, the cue ball goes on the head spot.
- If an object ball is made in the wrong pocket, it's spotted on the foot spot, or as near to it as possible, directly behind it (behind means towards the foot rail).
- When the shooter has ball in hand behind the head string and all of the object balls are also behind the head string, the object ball nearest this line may be spotted upon request on the foot spot. If there's a tie between two balls, the shooter can chose which one he wants spotted.
- If the 14th and 15th balls are pocketed on the same stroke, the balls are reracked.
  Note: This isn't an opening break shot, you don't have to drive two balls to the rail.

Foul versus legal shots   As in 8-ball and 9-ball, a failure to satisfy the requirements of a legal shot results in a foul. In 14.1, however, to add insult to injury, you're docked one point for each foul. And yes, it's possible for a player to have a negative score.

Three successive fouls   In 9-ball if a player commits three consecutive fouls, this results in an automatic loss of game. Committing three successive fouls in 14.1 will cost you points. If he fouls, the shooter loses one point. Whether you're keeping score on a piece of paper or a chalkboard, the scorer notes that the shooter is "on a foul."

On the shooter's next turn at the table, if she pockets a called ball or executes a legal safety, the foul notation is removed. Remember a miss only means a loss of turn. If the shooter fouls again, she loses another point and the note is revised to "on two fouls." Three times unlucky – on the third consecutive turn at the table, a foul results in another one point penalty plus an extra 15 points, which wipes the slate clean.

The incoming player now has the choice of playing the balls as they lie or having all 15 balls reracked. The offending player shoots again. Should the offending player scratch on the break, she loses a point and goes back to being "on one foul."

Chapter Eight

Bar pool survival

As popular as it is, bar pool has garnered a poor reputation among certain pool purists as the black sheep of the billiard family. Some players, with even less compassion – if that's possible – disown the game entirely: "It's just not pool."

There are reasonable arguments behind this blatant disregard for bar 8-ball as it's traditionally been played on the coin-operated table. For the most part, many players argue that the equipment is substandard and poorly maintained. The oversized or weighted cue ball that facilitates the internal vending and ball return system for the coin-op table offers a phony reaction. Moreover, the unofficial rules, which vary from bar to bar, allow players to play illegal safeties and fouls without a fair penalty.

Amateur 8-ball leagues are changing the weathered face of bar pool. They're racking up and educating more and more members and are attracting big-name sponsors. The fun, new friends and camaraderie of regular league activity make pool nights the highlight of many players' week. If you enjoy bar pool, join a league. You'll be instantly adopted into a fun-loving family that extends across North America.

EQUIPMENT

The coin-operated table   Designed originally for any place with limited space, the coin-operated pool table has become a popular staple of most bars and clubs, precisely why players began to call it a **bar box**. The compact 3½ x 7 ft. is most commonly found in bars and billiard clubs that host amateur 8-ball league play; a fancier 4 x 8 ft. model with fringed leather pockets graces many upscale establishments.

There are two main differences between a commercial pocket billiards table and bar box. The playing surface of a regulation pocket billiards table is made up of three separate pieces of slate, the slate of a small coin-op is one complete sheet of slate. Also, more noticeably, the coin-op – like a washer or dryer in a laundromat – has been manufactured with a vending system. You have to feed anywhere from 50 cents to $2.50 into push coin slides to play.

There's a **ball return system** inside every coin-op: a labyrinth of shutes and troughs direct the pocketed numbered balls into a locked Plexiglas-covered storage area. A **separator** distinguishes the cue ball from the numbered balls, then diverts it into its own cue ball return area.

A new and visionary table (ball return) system is working its way into bars and clubs. This table has an internal sensor that reads the optical density of the numbered balls and the cue-ball. As soon as the white ball, which has a much higher optical density, passes by, it's kicked into a separate cue-ball return area. This system allows bar players to compete using a cue ball that's the same size and weight as the numbered balls, and under a much-improved standard of playing conditions.

The bar ball   With the intricate ball return system of a coin-operated table came the invention of the bar cue ball: a necessary evil. For the vending and ball return system to work, the cue ball was traditionally manufactured with physical differences. It's bigger, smaller, heavier, lighter or manufactured with magnetic character-istics. All of these bar balls share one key similarity: they complicate your shot making. Ball reaction suffers greatly because of these distinguishing characteristics. To play winning bar pool, you must make certain adjustments.

Playing with a weighted and oversized cue ball

- To get the feel for the oversized cue ball, at medium speed, shoot it at an object ball with a little draw five times. Now switch the balls around. Shoot the same shot five times using the smaller numbered ball as the cue ball and the oversized bar ball as the object ball. This will help you to appreciate the relationship between the balls.
- If you can avoid it, never hit a weighted or oversized cue ball

softly over a distance. The extra weight can make the cue ball rock – not roll – and wreck havoc with your positional strategy.

- When shooting with an oversized cue ball, you must compensate for the ball's extra size in your aim. The basic formula for calculating the point of aim – aiming the center of the cue ball into the center of the ghost ball – remains the same. However, don't forget to visualize an oversized ghost ball; you must adjust your point of aim accordingly.

- On rail shots, if the object ball is frozen to the rail, aim the oversized bar ball to contact the rail first just a hair before the object ball. A little outside English also gets the job done, especially if you must shoot the object ball the length of the rail past the side pocket.

- Center-ball hits are always your best bet. The effects of spin, draw and stop are more difficult to achieve and predict with an oversized cue ball. Miscues are more likely. Follow becomes easier. Try to play a position where you must follow the cue ball instead of drawing. Look for a pattern with natural angles: avoid going to the rail to play position wherever possible.

- On a draw shot, it's important to note that the oversized cue ball is likely to move forward before moving back. Take this into consideration when playing a shot that requires pinpoint position.

- The effects of follow are more pronounced with an oversized cue ball. On all shots, be conscious of cue speed. A weighted cue ball will transfer more power to the object ball. Always consider the path of the cue ball after contact, as scratching becomes easier. You can still hit the ball firmly and maintain control by hitting the cue ball a hair lower than usual on every shot.

- Caroms and billiards can be easier to make with an oversized cue ball because of the increased surface area.

- On a center-ball hit, the path of the oversized cue ball may alter slightly after contact from the traditional right-angle line; expect the cue ball to depart on an angle that's a little less than the standard 90°. Adjust accordingly.

Beating the bar box   Playing winning pool on a beat-up bar table relies on the understanding that the conditions are the same for both you and your opponent. If you want to win, stay calm and stay aware. The player who learns to use the table's idiosyncrasies to advantage will have an invaluable edge.

Do

✔ *Read the rolls.* Before you begin, roll a ball from corner to corner and side to side. Take note of any drifts or rolls. If this is the case, you'll have to adjust your aim and hit.

✔ *Play the rolls.* If the table rolls in, sometimes your margin of error increases greatly as the drift can carry an off-target ball into the pocket. If the table rolls out, avoid soft hits and/or adjust your aim.

✔ *Use the flaws.* If a table, structural beam, mirror or other bar furniture obstructs one side of the table, it's a smart tactic to leave the cue ball there for your opponent.

✔ *Be physically flexible*. When space is a problem, you won't have the luxury of assuming the perfect textbook stance. Some players are quick to reveal their indignation. They pound the impeding wall with the butt of their cue, or shove a table angrily as if to say, "See, this is why I will miss." Wise bar players prefer to direct their energy into finding a balanced – if slightly unorthodox – stance that gets the cue through straight. Don't get frustrated. If you want to pocket an awkward shot, you'll need to stay extra still on your delivery.

Don't

✘ *Hammer the butt* of your cue into a jammed coin slide. This will only cause more damage. Report the problem to the owner or manager and ask for a refund.

✘ *Pick up a bar box* and drop it to move it or disengage hung-up balls. This can wreck the table – and your back.

✘ *Stuff the pockets* with napkins, cigarette cartons or a drink. Pocketed balls will eventually push this debris into the troughs and jam up the works.

✘ *Push the cue* into various parts of the table to trigger the ball release. Coin-op manufacturers have outsmarted cheaters: this no longer works.

8-BALL VERSUS 8-BRAWL

Unfortunately there will always be pool school drop-outs – bar players who refuse to learn how to play nicely. Avoid these people; their contests are seldom about pool. If the bar tables are full of bad actors, your best move is always a quick exit.

Any player who dismisses a legal safety shot in 8-ball as "dirty pool," is a bar-taught clown. Played properly, 8-ball is a defensive game. Played legally, safeties are highly skilled shots.

Never chase a loss. If you're playing players who are floating the cue ball in and out of tight positions for perfect position on their next shots, missing key balls by a conspicuously small margin or missing and leaving the cue ball perfect on your next shot, they're probably hustling. Either play for fun, make another game that evens the playing field or take your lumps and quit.

Bar rules for 8-ball   Some bar pool players can get very testy and territorial about their ideas of how the game of 8-ball should be played. If you're looking to challenge a stranger – particularly on their home table – it's customary to play by house rules. As there are so many variations, be smart: talk before you chalk. Here are some options of play to agree on before your runouts turn into run-ins.

The break   Do four balls have to go to the rail? If the 8-ball drops, is it an automatic win? If the 8-ball and the cue ball fall on the same stroke, is that an automatic loss? If the 8-ball and another ball drop, is it a win or a loss? If a numbered ball is legally pocketed on the break, is it still open table or are you automatically committed to that group?

Fouls   Are you playing call shots or call pocket? If you make your ball and your opponents', is that a loss of turn? Are airborne numbered balls respotted (and where) or do they stay down?

Penalties   Your opponent fouls. Do you take cue ball in hand anywhere on the table and shoot in any direction, or behind the line and shoot at balls up table?

Losses   The 8-ball flies off of the table; you make the 8-ball and your opponent's ball; the 8-ball is sunk too soon or in the wrong pocket; you hit the 8-ball first when it wasn't your legal object ball; you pocket the cue ball and the 8-ball in the same stroke; you hook yourself on the 8-ball and then fail to hit it. Is it all over but the crying? Fouls on the 8-ball are well worth discussing before the opening break.

Jump shots   Let your opponent know ahead of time that you know the difference between a legal jump shot and a scoop. Jabbing the cue under the cue ball and lifting it into the air is a foul. (And good luck trying to legally jump a weighted ball with a butt-heavy house cue.)

SHARK ATTACK!

Outhustling a hustler   Hustlers love bar pool. Why? Because sharks are attracted to chum bags – and bars are full of them. A hustler is a predator, a competitive pool player that's also a skilled actor, psychologist and opportunist.

Hustlers know exactly who they're looking for – "bad investors". These are opponents carrying cash (no credit) who have never really seen a great player and overrate their own game. Hustlers adore "go-offs": emotional players who are easy to "get down." These players tend not to quit when beaten: rather, they chase their losses. And hustlers know how to press all the right buttons.

Quality hustling involves hiding true speed – or skill level. Hustlers will commonly weaken their break; use a goofy bridge; alter their stroke; play left-handed; pocket balls being careful not to spin the rock (the cue ball); and lie about their identity. They play clever two-way shots and make key safety or breakout shots look like a fluke.

They intentionally miss so that they can position the cue ball in a spot that forces you to take a shot they want you to make. They can read the table like a Dr. Seuss book. In fact, there's only one thing even the greatest hustler cannot do, and that's beat an honest man!

Beat or be beaten – How to swim with the sharks You finally realize, after a few racks, that your opponent's a shark. So, what are you going to do? Chase your loss? Quit? Or get psyched to kick some guppy butt?

The first step to beating a better player is to admit that you can't – then create the game you can. Here are some 8-ball handicapping gems designed to give you the swimming edge:

- They have to shoot the 1 to 10 balls, while you play the 11 to 15.
- They must shoot the 8-ball in the same pocket as their first or last pocketed ball.
- They must play their balls into one pocket or the pockets on one side of the table.
- They must shoot all of their balls in order.
- They must bank the 8-ball or every ball to win (great edge on a table with dead rails).
- They must play one or two cushion position on every shot.

AMATEUR POOL LEAGUES

Joining an amateur pool league is a great way to meet people and mentors, learn new skills and take your game to the next level. Not only can you play on a team made up of both men and women with varying skill levels or handicaps, but you can watch some jam-up pool players in action!

While some bars and clubs organize their own in-house leagues, others are hooked up with a national 8-ball association. In addition to regular team play, these leagues offer cash payouts, trophies and a shot at playing your way to the championships, which are held annually in Las Vegas. Imagine a hotel ballroom featuring rows and rows of tables, top 8-ballers from all over North America and around-the-clock pool events: it's quite a party!

Each 8-ball league will have its own format. The handicapping systems will also vary. If you're looking for some fun, casual competition, you may want to join a league that permits flukes in regular-season play. In an effort to attract newcomers, these leagues purposely soften the rules. By finding ways to franchise the element of luck, they get more participation at the grass roots level and keep their newcomers hooked on pool.

If you're the type of player who likes it tough, preferring a format that shows no special clemency, join a league that upholds the official "called shot" rules. While you'll probably have to take a few lumps in the beginning, these formats will turn you into a much better player in the long run.

Chapter Nine

Winning pool

While pool requires solid shot-making ability, you can't play to win without tenacity and a composed competitive temperament. There are practice drills in Chapter 11, aimed at strengthening your cue and cue ball control, but the mental discipline that pool demands at this level of play can only come from applied effort.

If you strive to elevate your own personal standard of excellence every time you pick up a cue, then you'll always be playing winning pool. Learn to channel and play through nerves and adrenaline, manage anger and frustration, reject negative thoughts and block out distractions at the table. Overcoming these problems is an immensely satisfying part of the journey for players armed with a winning attitude.

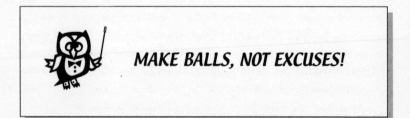

MAKE BALLS, NOT EXCUSES!

TEN PRINCIPLES OF WINNING POOL

1. **Competition**   If you want to improve, play better players. Test your skills and your courage under varying degrees of pressure. To get stronger you need to face your weaknesses – how else will you know what areas of your game need work?

    Don't let fear of losing to a better player stop you from entering a local tournament. First of all, most amateur tournaments are handicapped, which gives you a good shot at challenging more experienced players. But most importantly, you give yourself a chance to watch and learn from those better players. Skilled opponents should inspire, not intimidate.

    Instead of worrying about what you look like or what others must think, dig your toes in and just play to the best of your ability. And, should you lose, take the spoils of defeat on to the practice table. As legendary football coach Vince Lombardi said, "It's not whether you get knocked down, it's whether you get up."

2. **Commitment**   Make all necessary decisions before you get down over a ball. This involves reading the table, selecting a shot or strategy and determining how you will execute the shot. Where will you hit the cue ball? At what speed? Will you be altering anything in your stroke: moving your bridge closer, moving your grip up or down? Where is the cue ball going after contact? Could you scratch? Could a blocking ball interfere with your positional play?

    Flubbed shots occur because players are still thinking while pulling the trigger. When this happens, your brain sends a confused set of commands to your stroking arm. Miscues, a badly timed hit or body English (moving on the shot) are common results. If your brain is still grinding, get up and regroup. Once you're down on the shot, commit to it.

3. **Confidence**   The English poet John Milton understood that "the mind is its own place, and in itself can make a heaven of hell, and a hell of heaven." Thoughts are deeds! Negative thoughts can manifest physically in a tense stroking arm. If your confidence, for reasons real or imagined, deserts you mid-match, get it back using the following popular techniques:

Positive visualization   Before you get down on the shot, see the object ball travelling along its path to drop successfully in the intended pocket. Take a few deep breaths. Feel your confidence build. It will flow down through your stroking arm, loosening your shoulder and arm, and charge your grip.

Power phrases   Try silently repeating a word or a phrase to yourself, something that has the power to fire your competitive spirit, or invoke calm or a feeling of invincibility. Nike's "Just do it," or "No fear" are examples.

Adjusting your attitude and goals   You'll save yourself a lot of aggravation if you can just accept that there will be many strange twists of fate in a game of pool. Enjoy the ride. Opponents miss their shots and hook you or fluke their game ball. You can miss your shape by an eighth of an inch and hook yourself. Your opponent got the balls moving and now the table's a dog's breakfast. When the going gets touch, embrace the challenge. If your focus is directed to problem-solving, there's no energy left for self-doubt or self-pity.

4. **Self-control**   If you miss a key shot, or are having one of those sessions where you can't seem to make a ball, resist the temptation to "go off." Smacking the edge of the table, throwing chalk or your cue or resorting to demoralizing theatrics is a colossal waste of focus. In addition to empowering your opponent and looking extremely foolish in the process, there's a much more important reason to keep your pool cool.

   A miss always yields valuable information about your stance and stroke, a particular shot or the playing conditions. Did the table roll? Did the ball take a weird turn after it passed over the seam in the slate? Did you put unintentional siding on the cue ball? Did you get a kick? Did you turn your wrist again? Was the contact on the object ball too thick or thin? Was your aim off? If you're too busy carrying on like a toddler who just dropped an ice cream cone, you can't possibly figure anything out.

5. **Intent**   When you visit the table, don't just get up and take a turn. Have a purpose with every trip. Analyze the table, review your options and look for the smartest shot under the circumstances.

6. **Humility**   Even world champions know to expect the unexpected in pool, which is why they never take unnecessary chances. Even if you're playing a first time starter, never underestimate your opponent. The tables can turn very quickly. If you're playing to win, always play your best game – regardless of your opponent's skill level.

7. **Concentration**   You will need to block out two kinds of distractions when playing. Internal distractions are quite possibly the worst – because they come from you. Just as you settle down into your shot a horrible inner voice will say: "Boy, are you ever gonna look like a loser when you miss this!" That is, if it isn't torturing you with some unrelated nonsense or sore points of an intensely personal nature. Listen to or spar with this demon id and presto: you have more than one opponent at the table.

    A loud spectator, whistling waiter or wheezy opponent: these are examples of external distractions. The minute you become aware of them, your momentum at the table is already destroyed. And when you lose concentration, a whisper will seem like a scream. Your agitation wells. You start popping up on your shots. Your stroking arm rejects all of your instructions. What's worse (the voice inside will probably point out) is that you now have a perfectly reasonable excuse for losing. What can you do?

    • Silently, yell at your id: "Stop! Enough! Shut up!"
    • Override the negative voice with a positive message. "You can't make this" becomes "This ball's going down!"
    • Shepherd all of the distracting noises into one big imaginary room in your head. Imagine that you've just had a dimmer installed. Now, slowly fade it down … and out.
    • Get back into the game and stay there. When your opponent is at the table, don't let your mind wander. Focus on how you might play the shot the opposing player is about to shoot.

8. **Opponents**   There are opponents who go about the business of pocketing balls with dignity, integrity and skill. They give up the table when they lose, which means they

accept that their turn is over and allow you to play your game without any insidious interference. They win and lose graciously. Pay homage to these opponents for they are thoroughbreds. For all others, remember, play the game, not the player. Focus on what it takes to put a ball into a pocket and position the cue ball.

9. **Winning habits**   If you lose a game on a miss, don't unscrew your cue and walk away from the table. If you can, set the shot back up and hit it until you own it. Always leave on a positive note, confident that you'll make it the next time it comes up.

- Avoid the buffet before you play. (You're heading to a pool table, not the electric chair.) Heavy meals can curb your concentration. Eat lightly and you'll be hungry to win.

- Before a match, hit easy shots with the intent of warming up your stroking arm and building confidence. This is not the time to practice. You also want to loosen up your mind. Some players listen to music, others play video games to dull their minds and induce a trance-like state before they play. Find the trick that works for you.

10. **Perspective**   If you're losing confidence and getting nervous, it helps to remember that pool is just a game. Formula One racers say, "Avoid distraction or end up in traction." The great thing about pool is that you're not taking sharp turns at 200 km/h. If you make an error in a tournament, the worst thing that can happen, realistically, is that a ball doesn't fall into a pocket. You'll get 'em next time!

COMBATING NERVES

When you shoot a ball that means a lot to you, there is a tendency to lose focus and put too much pressure on yourself. Nerves can envelop you like a cloud, rendering you temporarily incapable of seeing and shooting straight. Here are some tips to help tame those tremors

Keep the edge   If you're not a little nervous before you play, chances are you're not really up to the match anyway. Some players believe that they play better after a few drinks. Wrong! Alcohol isn't a relaxant: it's a depressant. Even if it gets you through the first few games, it can leave you drained and dull-witted just when you need energy and clarity the most. You're far better off letting your nerves work for you.

Exercise Sweating away from the table can increase your energy at the table and burn away mental cobwebs.

Surf the alpha waves Relax your mind and the body follows. Learn to breathe deeply from the lower part of the lungs as this produces brain waves that are linked to relaxation. Place one hand on your stomach. Relax your shoulders and breathe, concentrating on expanding and contracting your stomach and the back of your waist only. Your chest should remain relatively still. Inhale through your nose and exhale through your mouth.

Dress for success Short skirts, low tops, tight or hard shoes, high heels, cowboy boots and restrictive clothes can hinder your balance, mood and ability to execute certain shots. Wear classy but comfortable clothes, something that won't add to the already hemmed-in feeling that high-pressure sessions can create.

Don't give up Nerves are temporary. Force yourself to play through them. If you're shooting a key ball and your heart is pounding and your bridge hand shaking, get up. Walk around the table. Rechalk. Breathe. Review the shot. Get back down – and just do it!

Self-awareness Develop a checklist of things to do when you're playing through nerves. This can include helpful reminders such as slow down, shorten your backstroke, keep your head still while shooting, don't pull the trigger until you're sure, let the cue go and relax, silly, there's nothing to fear but fear itself.

Reasonable expectations Examples of unrealistic expectations include: I will win today. I will crush my opponent. Not even a living legend has control over that. This kind of thinking produces an unmanageable amount of pressure. As a player, the only thing that you can reasonably expect to do is to give each shot your best. Concentrate on making one ball correctly and the runs will take care of themselves.

Practice, practice, practice Nerves usually occur because you lack confidence in your game. There's simply nothing that can bridle a runaway pulse like the knowledge that you've done your homework.

DEADSTROKING VERSUS CHOKING

Being in "deadstroke" is a pool expression that describes a state of absolute focus. It's a surreal condition where, without any conscious effort, you pocket every ball you shoot at. Your awareness is heightened but you are deeply relaxed. Your cue seems to be guided by a benign force and, in this state of grace, everything you have ever learned about the game of pool just suddenly shows up. In fact, players in deadstroke rarely know how they ran out; it usually only occurs to them as their game ball finds the dead center pocket like a homing pigeon.

When you're in deadstroke, this blissfully blank state just happens – it's not something you can command. However, if you're practicing regularly, and can enter a session with perfect faith that the basics of stance and stroke are working like a well-oiled machine, this condition is far more likely to occur. These moments will keep you inexorably hooked on pool.

Choking, on the other hand, is an all-too-common phenomenon that may drive you to want to quit pool and take up lawn darts. A miss is a miss, but when a player seizes up under pressure and flubs a key shot because of it, this is referred to in the pool circles as choking or, "dogging your brains out."

All players have gone through slumps where they can't seem to break this seemingly addictive habit. When this happens, the first step is to just call it something else. Competitive snooker players attribute this error to what it really is – a loss of concentration. This seems a lot more manageable than the queasy feeling that you're missing because of some deep-seated psychosomatic flaw. If you're not feeling your indomitable self, try shortening your backstroke and concentrating on going through the cue ball until you find deadstroke.

Chapter Ten

Winning practice

Practice is the only way to improve cue and cue ball control, build confidence and find the eye of the hurricane under pressure. While knocking balls around randomly or playing a friend isn't as dull as drills, it's also not practice. You can't possibly derive the same benefits as from a few hours of hitting balls according to specific goals.

If you play often but have trouble committing to a regular practice routine, consider this: setting up the same drill and hitting the same ball over and over again can be a bit boring, but it's infinitely more enjoyable than losing, isn't it? Practice to win!

A PRACTICE PARADIGM

Practice regularly Even if you can't dedicate as much time as a pro or top amateur, your game will still improve with a few focused hours a week of practice. In the beginning, regular sessions yield greater results than longer but less frequent sessions.

Practice by yourself If anyone comes to your table and wants to chat, blow them off nicely: you have homework.

Practice with purpose Set goals for yourself, and work on one thing at a time. Trying to take on too much can be overwhelming and dispiriting.

Practice – only if you want to practice If you're hitting balls and your heart's not in it, you're only reinforcing weaknesses. Be eager to play, and try your best on every shot.

STANCE AND STROKE DRILLS

Stance and stroke   Practice stroking your cue – smoothly – in and out of the mouth of a (dry) beer or soda bottle. Feather the center of the bottle opening, pause, and pull the cue back slowly, (or pull the cue back slowly and pause), then release the cue into the mouth and through to the back of the bottle. Repeat, being careful to keep your stroke fluid and a consistent rhythm. After about 20 strokes, get up. Walk away. Set up again and practice another set of 20 strokes.

Follow-through or finish   To test your follow-through, set up the cue ball and another ball (call this your position ball) side by side, but not touching. Stroke the cue ball into a corner pocket, and don't move until your cue comes to a natural stop. Check to see how much cue shaft is in front of the position ball. If the tip of your cue is just peering over your bridge hand and barely past the position ball, you'll have to make adjustments to your grip and stance. Typically, you want to see six to eight inches of cue shaft.

 Use self-adhesive vinyl hole reinforcements to mark the original positions of the cue ball and the object ball, or the spot where *whitey* stops. This makes it possible to practice the same shot over and over again. They peel off easily; don't leave messy marks (like chalk) and are pool cloth-friendly.

CENTER AND NON-CENTER BALL DRILLS

Center-ball drills   Using medium speed, aim the cue ball at the center of the foot rail (middle diamond). Stay down on your shot. If you're doing everything correctly, the cue ball will come back along a straight line and hit the tip of your cue. If the cue ball isn't striking the center of the foot rail before rebounding, there's a flaw in your stance, stroke or aim. Place a matchstick in the middle, on the edge of the cushion and try knocking it off. If the cue ball contacts the matchstick but still rebounds to the left or right of center, you've put unintentional English on the cue ball. Try this drill 10 times, or until you can make the cue ball go up and down the center spots.

Now add an object ball. Place a second ball in the middle of the table. Strike the center of the cue ball at medium speed. The cue ball will hit this object ball to the foot rail. The object ball should come back down the table and kiss the cue ball along the same line.

Try using a striped ball as your cue ball. Place it on the table with the stripe running horizontally. Hit the ball at medium speed and watch the stripe after it grabs the cloth. Is it still horizontal? Or is it revolving to the right or to the left? Hit it a few more times. If it's still winding its way right or left – and you still swear that you're hitting dead center – you could have a dominant eye. You're not alone. Many top players have learned to compensate for this irregularity by moving their cue tip a "hair" in the opposite direction on every shot.

Straight-in shot drills   Another great drill for improving your stance and stroke is to place a ball (8-ball or 9-ball) on the center spot. Position the cue ball along or behind the head string so that you have a long straight-in shot into either the right or left corner pocket. Play the shot using a medium hard stroke, with a half a tip below center. If you hit it perfectly, the cue ball isn't breathing or spinning: it stops dead in its tracks. If you didn't, the cue ball will have drifted to the right or left. If this is happening with alarming regularity, freeze after you finish the shot and take a look at your cue. Is it pointing into the corner pocket? If not, your cue's coming off-line. Keep a personal record of how many of these shots you can make in a row and keep trying to beat your personal best.

Full-to-fine cut shots   Position the object ball one diamond from the corner pocket, about 2 cm off the side or long rail (mark the spot). Begin with a straight-in shot: place your cue ball three diamonds from the corner pocket, and using a center ball hit, sink your object ball into the corner. Gradually move your cue ball (a full ball's width) away from the rail, thereby slowly increasing the angle of the shot. Keep cutting your object ball in until your cue ball is near the side pocket and make sure to observe the path of the cue ball after contact.

Rail shot drill   Freeze one ball on the cushion in front of each of the 12 diamonds or spots. Place the cue ball in the center of the table and in any order, begin making all 12 balls. If you miss a shot, put it back to its original position and keep shooting.

Pressure position play Take three balls – the 7-, 8-, and 9-ball – and roll them randomly on the table (mark their positions). The objective of this drill is to pretend that you're on the hill (tied with your opponent) in the world 9-ball championship. Your opponent has just scratched, giving you ball in hand and a chance to win the world title and the million-dollar prize purse. Your mission, should you choose to accept it, is to run out.

Analyze the position of the balls. Come up with a game plan. How will you make the 7-ball to get on the 8-ball, and the 8-ball to get on the 9-ball? Try and run out. If you miss, or lose position, set the balls up again. If you're successful, try a slightly different pattern: there's always more than one way to play position.

Make this drill interesting by turning it into a challenge with another player. Play a set of 10 random runouts for a small wager. Not only will this test of mettle increase your motivation and concentration, but it will allow you to watch how another player executes the same runout.

Precision stop, draw and follow shot drills

This consists of three separate drills to practice precision stun, draw and follow at varying distances.

To practice your **stop shot**, begin by lining up a straight-in shot with your object ball at point A, a few centimetres off the side rail, one diamond from the corner pocket and your cue ball at point B, at the side pocket. Now, using a below center hit, stop your rock at point A. Then gradually move your cue ball back to point C, and point D. It will become increasingly more difficult to stop the cue ball at point A. Remember that in order to stop the cue ball at varying distances, you will have to adjust your speed and below-center hit. If you miss, or the cue ball drifts or is spinning on the cloth, take the shot over. If you really want to improve, keep shooting the shot until you can stop it perfectly at least three times. For a tougher challenge, move the cue ball back to point E.

Now practice your **draw shot**. Place your object ball at point A and your cue ball at point B. Begin by pocketing your object ball into the corner and drawing your cue ball to points B, D, and then to the rail. Now, keep your object ball at point A and place your cue ball at point C. Draw the cue ball back to the end rail. When you can do this three times, move the cue ball back to points D and E and try to draw the cue ball, still at point A, to the end rail. The farther the distance between the cue ball and the object ball, the more expert your stroke must be. At this stage this becomes an advanced drill.

The last leg of this circuit works your **follow shot**. With the cue ball at point D and your object ball at point B, using follow, sink the object ball in the corner pocket. Practice leaving the cue ball at point A after contact. Repeat the shot, but this time *follow* the cue ball into the same pocket.

Next, try a series with the cue ball at points E, D and C. Again follow the cue ball to Point A first, then into the corner pocket.

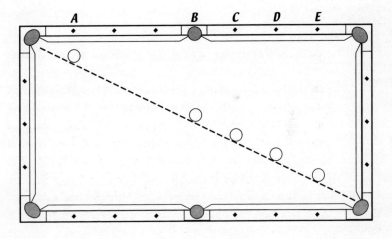

Appendix One

Pool rules in a nutshell

Recognized as the sanctioning body for pocket billiards in North America, the Billiards Congress of America (BCA) publishes the *Official Rules and Records Book*. Based on the *BCA General Rules of Pocket Billiards*, here are some of the more useful rules in a nutshell. Note: The penalties for fouls will differ depending on the game you're playing (you'll find rulings relevant to particular games in Chapter 7).

Opening break
- The opening break is shot with the cue ball "in hand" anywhere behind the head string. Once the tip has struck the cue ball, it's officially showtime! If the cue ball is deflected or stopped after it crosses the head string on the opening break, this is a foul and loss of turn. The opponent can either receive the cue ball behind the head string or assign the break back to the offending player.
- On the opening break, if the shot fails to contact a legal object ball in the rack or drive the cue ball over the head string, the shot is a foul and the opponent receives the choice to take or give the break back to the offending player.

Legal shots
- A shot is legal if it causes the cue ball to contact a legal object ball and pockets a numbered ball, or it causes the cue ball or any numbered ball to hit a cushion after the cue ball has contacted a legal object ball.
- If extra balls are pocketed on a legal stroke, they count.

Spooked, spun and bounced balls

- If a ball shimmies, shifts or moves by itself, the ball stays where it is and play is resumed. If a ball has been hanging over a hole for less than five seconds and it drops it's considered pocketed. If it drops after five seconds or longer, it's placed back into its original position and play resumes.

- If a ball drops into a pocket on a legal stroke, this is considered a pocketed ball. If it drops out of a ball return pocket and onto the floor, it's still pocketed. However, if it falls into a pocket and the pocket spits it out, this is not a pocketed ball. The shooter loses his turn.

- Balls that bounce and roll along the rails and the cushion tops are legal, providing they return to the playing surface (or find a pocket) without touching anything that is not a part of the table (such as a light fixture, cube of chalk or player's hand). If the ball flies and lands off the table or returns to the table bed after caroming a foreign object, it's considered a ball that's jumped off the table, and a foul. (In 8-ball and 9-ball, these numbered balls are not put back in play. They are spotted in straight pool.)

Fouls versus loss of turn

- On a legal stroke, if a player doesn't pocket the legal object ball, the result is a loss of turn.

- A player must have at least one foot on the floor at the moment the tip contacts the cue ball, or the shot is a foul.

- If the cue ball fails to make contact with any legal object ball, this is a foul.

- If a ball is not pocketed, failure to cause the cue ball or a numbered ball to hit a cushion, after the cue ball has contacted a legal object ball, is a foul.

- If on a stroke the cue ball is pocketed (scratched), this is a foul. If the cue ball even touches a pocketed ball, as when the pocket is full, this is a foul shot.

- It's a foul to contact the cue ball or object balls in play with anything other than the cue tip. This includes a player's body or clothing, the cue shaft or equipment such as chalk or loose bridge heads. (The unofficial ruling regarding replacing an object ball that's been moved accidentally is that the offending player can't restore the moved ball back to its original position or it's a foul. The offending player must first ask the opponent if he wants it moved back or not).

- While placing a cue ball that you have in hand, touching an object ball is a foul.
- If the cue stick strikes the cue ball more than once on a shot, this is called a double hit and is a foul.
- If the cue stick remains on the cue ball for a suspicious length of time, this is considered a push shot and it's a foul. (Also, if the cue ball and the object ball are very close together, to avoid a push shot, the player must elevate the cue shaft and strike the cue ball so that these balls are not travelling in the same direction at the same speed. Or the player must shoot the ball so that the cue ball travels in another direction.)
- Marking the table (with a cube of chalk, coin or other marker) in any way that assists in the execution of a shot, is a foul. Nor is a player allowed to use a device to gauge whether or not the cue ball has enough room to roll through a gap. Players can hold their cues above a shot to determine distance or align a shot.

Spotting balls

- A spotted ball (or balls) is replaced on the long string: a single ball is spotted on the foot spot, and additional balls are spotted on the long string in numerical sequence "beginning on the foot spot and advancing toward the foot rail." Often there will be an interfering ball or balls on the foot spot or around the long string. If this is the case, spotted balls are then placed behind the foot spot (toward the foot rail) on the long string as close as possible (frozen if need be) to the interfering balls. The exception to this rule is if the interfering ball is the cue ball. Never freeze a spotted ball against the cue ball; it must be spotted as near to the cue ball as possible without touching. In the case where there's no way to spot a ball on the long string behind the foot spot, it's spotted in front, on the long string (toward the center spot).

Appendix Two

Pool notes

When you see pros perform those unbelievable shots that you'd like to learn, reach for a pencil and write them down. Make some copies of the blank diagrams on the next pages to record the shots. Then practice or review that new break, spin shot or safety with an instructor. You'll find that taking pool notes will not only help you study the nuances of ball control, but also improve your memory and awareness at the table.

As in our sample below, record as much information as possible. Use the circle at the right to record where the cue tip hits the cue ball. Use the table markings on the rails as a guide to show ball movement. Your notes should record what the pictures don't show: speed of the hit, fullness of contact, etc.

Sample pool note

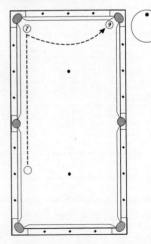

- *Use X-treme follow*
- *thick hit on the 7-ball*
- *medium pace (not too hard) and the cue ball billiards the 9-ball into the pocket!*

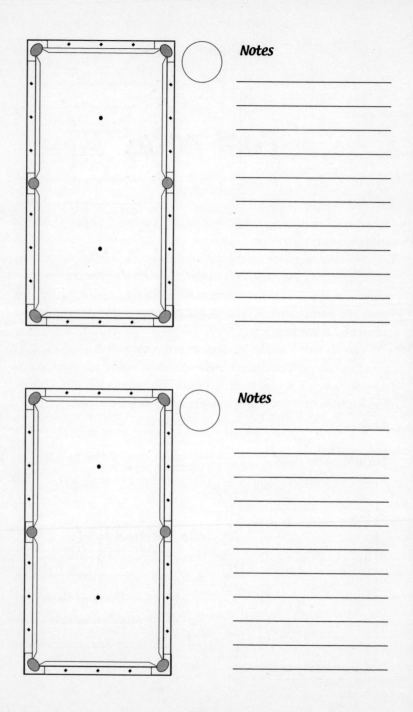

Notes

_____
_____
_____
_____
_____
_____
_____
_____
_____
_____

Notes

_____
_____
_____
_____
_____
_____
_____
_____
_____
_____

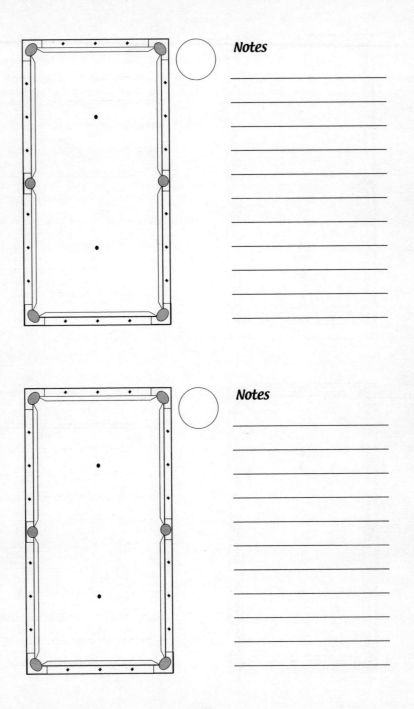

Notes

_____
_____
_____
_____
_____
_____
_____
_____
_____
_____
_____

Notes

_____
_____
_____
_____
_____
_____
_____
_____
_____
_____
_____

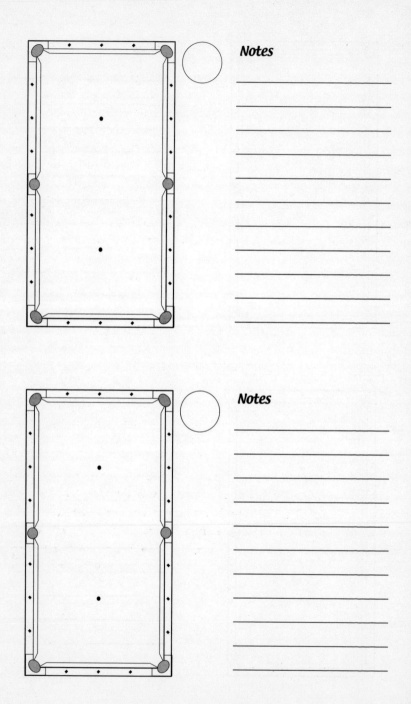

Notes

_____

_____

_____

_____

_____

_____

_____

_____

_____

_____

_____

Notes

_____

_____

_____

_____

_____

_____

_____

_____

_____

_____

_____

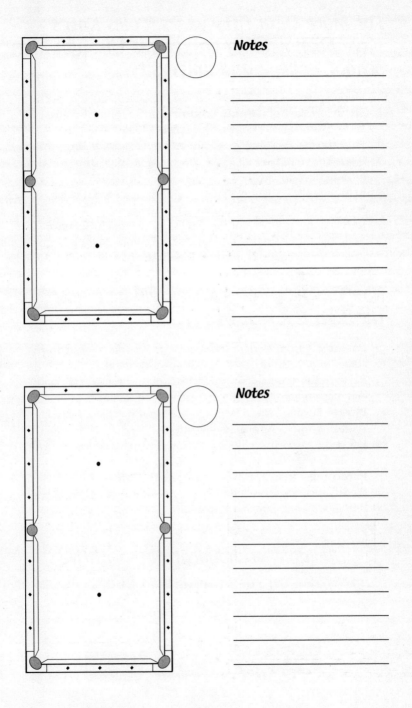

Notes

_____
_____
_____
_____
_____
_____
_____
_____
_____
_____
_____

Notes

_____
_____
_____
_____
_____
_____
_____
_____
_____
_____
_____

103

For more than fifty years, Coles Notes have been helping Canadians through high school, college and university...

- **Shakespeare** – all the famous plays explained, scene by scene
- **Shakespeare Total Study Editions** – includes the original play and a plain English version with scene-by-scene synopsis
- **Literature** – over sixty classic novels, from *Animal Farm* to *Wuthering Heights*, explained chapter-by-chapter with overviews by experts in the field
- **Senior Math** – six books from grade 11 topics to Calculus
- **Senior Science** – Physics, Chemistry, Biology
- **Reference** – from Senior English Essays to French Grammar
- **and still more titles** – *Canadian Law, Senior Accounting, American History, Economics, Advanced Spanish*

Now our _new_ Coles Notes will help you through the rest of life...

- **Business** – from *How to Write a Great Résumé* to *Start Your Own Small Business*, these books cover the field
- **Personal Finance** – covering stocks, mutual funds, real estate and many other topics to help manage your finances
- **Phrase Books** – seven language books for travellers, including Spanish, French, German and Japanese
- **Lifestyle** – over thirty titles covering gardening, sports and entertainment from *Better Golf* to *Speed Reading*
- **Parenting** – from *The First Year* to *Basketball for Kids*
- **Medical topics** – *Prostate Cancer, Breast Cancer, Thyroid Problems,* with many more to come.

Reliable, economical, authoritative information for Canadians ... Coles Notes

Coles Notes are available at ...